Petsitting Business

A step-by step guide to setting up a successful enterprise in this rapidly expanding market

Fiona Mackenzie

howtobooks

Published by How To Books Ltd,
Spring Hill House, Spring Hill Road,
Begbroke, Oxford OX5 1RX, United Kingdom
Tel: (01865) 375794, Fax: (01865) 379162
info@howtobooks.co.uk
www.howtobooks.co.uk

How To Books greatly reduce the carbon footprint of their books by
sourcing their typesetting and printing in the UK.

British Library Cataloguing in Publication Data
A catalogue record for this book is available from the British Library

ISBN 978 1 84528 289 9

Cover design by Baseline Arts Ltd, Oxford
Produced for How To Books by Deer Park Productions, Tavistock
Typeset by Pantek Arts Ltd, Maidstone, Kent.
Printed and bound by Cromwell Press Ltd, Trowbridge, Wilshire

NOTE: The material contained in this book is set out in good faith for
general guidance and no liability can be accepted for loss or expense
incurred as a result of relying in particular circumstances on statements
made in the book. Laws and regulation are complex and liable to change,
and readers should check the current position with the relevant authorities
before making personal arrangements.

CONTENTS

INTRODUCTION

Who would have thought that in just a few years, petsitting would become one of the fastest-growing industries in Britain today? From the nine-to-five professional to the globe-trotting family, hiring a petsitter has become as normal as using kennels or catteries.

I first heard of petsitting when I lived in Spain with my aunt who had set up a small business caring for the pets of British ex-pats who couldn't bring their pets with them on visits to their home country. Now, her business is in such demand that pet owners won't book their holidays unless they know she's free.

A few years after my return to England, I found myself with two children, a globe-trotting husband and two rescue dogs. Trying to leave for work every day was a disaster. I could hardly bear to look at the four sad faces at the window. So I decided to start up my own petsitting business in the early nineties, when hardly anyone had heard of petsitters and dog walkers.

It wasn't easy at first. There were no books I could read to tell me how to go about it properly and I didn't know any other petsitters to ask their advice. The internet was starting to grow but I didn't have a computer.

I made so many mistakes when I started my own business, so I decided to write this book so that I could share some of them with you – to save you making the same mistakes. I've learned the hard way and the great thing about petsitting is that you're constantly learning, about both pets and their owners. What I hadn't expected, however, was that my now wide circle of petsitting buddies would be so generous with their stories also. So as not to distract you from the information side of this book, I've added them after some of the chapters so you can read them at your leisure and laugh or commiserate with us.

This is a profession still in its infancy here with more and more pet owners looking for the perfect 'Mary Puppins' for their beloved pet. That person could be you!

ACKNOWLEDGEMENTS

I am very grateful to all the people who gave me their time and advice to help me write this book. In particular, I must thank:

Jane Wenham-Jones
Nikki Read
Lynne Patrick
Lane Mathias
Lynne Hackles
Tricia Maws
Gwen Bailey
Kris Glover, BA(Hons) DipCABT,
Fiona Strange, BSc BVetMed MRCVS
The veterinary nurses of Burghfield veterinary surgery
Andrea Gordon
Dianne Newell
Geoff Hogg
Denise Watson
Sophie Parker of PetPlan
Anne Mitchell of the Rabbit Welfare Association
Celia Haddon
Captain Black

My family, including Archie, Jessie and Bramble, my three rescue terriers and Mac the hamster and all the pets and their owners I've met over the past decade.

1
THE PROFESSION OF PETSITTING

In this chapter:

- ☐ Why petsitting is one of the fastest growing industries

- ☐ Deciding whether you could you be a petsitter

- ☐ Who uses petsitters?

- ☐ Is petsitting a pet lover's perfect career?

- ☐ Assessing your potential earnings

- ☐ Drawing up your petsitting business plan.

If you think of a job where you spend all day with pets, what comes to mind first? A vet? Apart from the gruelling seven-year training and the necessity of an unflinching attitude to blood and gore, you might find that the pets don't want to spend time with you. My vet once told me that she'd gone into the profession because she loved animals but the feeling obviously wasn't reciprocated. Dogs would cross the road if they saw her coming and cats would cower behind their owners in her surgery.

Petsitters, on the other hand, have the opposite effect. Dogs you walk will rush to greet you in the park, leaving their owners puffing in their wake. Cats sit vigilantly at windows, checking for your arrival and then tripping you up as they twine round your ankles.

Why petsitting is one of the fastest growing industries

Petsitting offers an alternative to kennels and catteries, which although may offer an excellent service, are not ideal for every pet, especially those who are used to sharing the sofa with their owners every night.

There is now a huge demand for knowledgeable, dedicated petsitters whose services have grown to include far more than the original, literal meaning of the word: 'petsitter'. *A pet sitter is a contracted service provider who takes care of a pet in its own home.* This is the definition given by www.babylon.com, an online dictionary and translation service. At the time of writing, I couldn't find 'pet sitter' or 'petsitter' in a British dictionary, which shows just how new this profession still is to the UK.

The following services are all ones which can be offered by a petsitter:

- ☐ pet day care

- ☐ pop-in visits

- ☐ overnight petsitting

- ☐ pet boarding

- ☐ dog walking

- ☐ puppy home visits

- ☐ dog crèches.

Any or all of these services are ones you can offer if you become a petsitter.

Deciding whether you could be a petsitter

My intention in writing this book was to try to offer as much information as I could, to anyone wanting to start up and run their own petsitting business. Generally, this is one person setting up as an independent sole trader or a couple of people going into it as a partnership. For anyone wanting to set up as an employer of petsitters – whether those petsitters are independent contractors or employees – my advice is to try it out as a smaller venture first, before committing yourself to the red tape and expense of becoming an employer.

Here are a few questions to ask yourself first:

☐ Do you not only love animals but are knowledgeable about those you'd like to care for? I do cover basic pet care in this book but you can build up your expertise further by reading the recommended books and asking the advice of other pet care professionals such as dog trainers, pet behaviourists, vets and fellow petsitters.

☐ If you're considering dog walking, are you happy to walk when the weather is freezing? Or if the rain is pouring down and you are sliding about on the mud with a couple of Jack Russells and a red setter who want to roll over and play in it? The flip side is walking in the park, watching your dogs leaping over logs and racing around just for the love of it. Or feeling the sun on your shoulders as you sit in a beautiful garden with a contented cat by your side, knowing your friends are stuck behind their office desks and perhaps feeling as bored as you were a few months ago.

☐ How reliable and committed are you? You cannot throw a 'sickie' when a puppy, two cats and six dogs are depending on you for food, walks and company. Colds and not feeling 100% won't wash with them. Of course you must always have a contingency plan in case you are really too sick to work, or need a break, and I will show you how to prepare one later on.

☐ Do you like people? I know this seems a strange question but sometimes petsitters start up with little or no people skills. After all, they may say: I work with animals now, why would I need to be good with people? It came as a surprise to me just how much I would be interacting with pet owners. I understood that there would be the telephone enquiry calls, the client consultations and perhaps a chat now and then to discuss their pets' needs or to change my visiting days. I didn't realize I'd soon be considered an expert on a bulldog's idiosyncrasies, or become second mother to an aging cat, nor did I think I'd be having long conversations about whether a raw food diet would be best for Tony, the great Dane, or if Charlotte, the spaniel, really needed a third fleecy coat.

☐ What family commitments do you have? If you are a parent, who will care for your children in the holidays? As a petsitter, your insurance won't cover them in the case of an accident or if they get bitten by a pet in your care, so you may need a support network. As petsitting is so flexible, there is nothing to stop you advertising your services as 'term time only' for dog walking, if you intend to include this service, and then caring for cats and small animals in the evening.

Who uses petsitters?

More and more people certainly are using petsitters. Hiring a petsitter is often considered a necessity and not a luxury. While kennels and catteries often offer excellent services, they are not ideal for every pet, especially those who are used to sharing the sofa with their owners every night.

Nowadays pet owners would no more leave their pet alone than they would a child. In the past, owners would ask neighbours, friends or family to care for their pets while they were at work or on holiday. People work very long hours, commuting times are longer, and relatives and friends are just as busy. It's become more difficult to find good care for our pets so if you have the expertise, reliability and dedication to care for pets and give owners peace of mind, you'll be very popular.

Is petsitting a pet lover's perfect career?

As a petsitter, I've had the privilege of meeting and spending my working days with a variety of wonderful animals. I've met the odd one of two who have been difficult but this has usually been because they've never been socialized, or because at some point in their lives a human has hurt them. With proper training and behavioural advice, these pets have all improved immeasurably.

For me, as a dedicated pet lover, petsitting has given me:

☐ The chance to be my own boss.

☐ An opportunity to learn about animal care, behaviour and training. This has been not only through being with animals every day but also by reading up on their care and meeting and learning from other pet professionals such as pet behaviourists, dog trainers, vets and veterinary nurses and other petsitters who are usually very generous with their advice.

☐ The opportunity to get fit! My own dogs have benefited from extra walks with some of the dogs I've walked and we've all got thinner and healthier from so much exercise.

Because of the contact with other pet professionals, petsitting can also be a stepping stone to careers in other animal-related industries. You have the opportunity to carve out your hours to completely suit you, your family, and, if you have them, your own pets. The biggest reward for me is to see the face in a window of a dog who's waiting for you to give him his walk and to be greeted with such affection when you step through the front door. Or to be able to cuddle a purring cat on a warm sofa after you've fed and groomed her.

It's not just the pets either. It's so rewarding to help a struggling mother whose dog is missing its long off-lead walks because she can't push her new baby's buggy in the woods. Or helping an elderly man who is too arthritic to take his dog out and being able to give his dog an exciting run in the park with a couple of doggy pals and a ball to chase.

As a dog walker, I've been instrumental in helping people who thought they couldn't take on a rescue dog, thereby providing a loving home for a dog who might have spent his entire life in a kennel. After a meeting or letter from me confirming that I am an insured petsitter, the rescue centres have allowed these people who would otherwise remain 'petless', to adopt a dog.

Assessing your potential earnings

It's not easy to put a figure on how much you can earn, apart from saying that the sky's the limit if you start off as a sole trader and then move up into recruiting your own pet-sitters and building a larger business.

Here are some examples that might help you consider thoroughly whether this is the profession for you. I wrote this as an article for the *Petsitting News* in July 2008 so bear in mind that the cost of living may have risen since then.

Example 1

Carol is a 43-year-old single mother to a 10-year-old daughter. Carol petsits from 9 a.m. to 3 p.m. on Mondays to Fridays. Back-up help if needed: Carol's mum.

Carol walks six dogs every morning in groups of three. In the afternoons, she walks four dogs, apart from Fridays when she has three extra. Carol doesn't look after cats and small animals. She is happy with the amount she has at the moment, but if she gets busier, she wants to employ a helper on a part-time basis.

Carol charges £10 per dog for a 40-minute walk and her weekly income is currently £650.

Example 2

Simon is 31 and is married with two young children. He's been petsitting for a year and works from 9 a.m. to 6 p.m.

Simon does five walks a day with four dogs in each walk at £10 per dog. He also offers pop-in visits for cats and has an average of three cat visits a day at £10 a visit. His current weekly income is approximately £1,150. In the summer his cat visits increase three-fold so he can earn up to £400 extra.

Example 3

Sarah is 36 and lives with her partner. They have three children, two of whom are under five. She only wants to work part time caring for cats. She has only been working for four months since March.

Since Sarah started advertising in the spring, she has quickly built up a small client base of 15 clients who are all going away for a couple of weeks' holiday between April and September. Sarah estimates she'll earn between £2,000 and £3,000 between April and the end of September. She hopes to have at least doubled her client base by next year and again the following year. After that her children will all be at school and she hopes to do some dog walking too.

Example 4

David, 55 and Helen, 49.

David took early retirement five years ago. He and Helen have been building up their petsitting business and haven't had to spend much on advertising because they are good friends of the local vet and have many retired friends who can afford to take frequent holidays and book Helen and David to care for their pets. Their friends have also recommended them to other friends.

Between them, they do 12 dog walks a day. They care for approximately ten cats a day in the winter and double this in the summer. David and Helen also offer a microchipping service and Helen has just passed her dog groomer's course. David is a qualified dog trainer and takes two classes every Saturday and one mid-week evening class. Because the business is growing so quickly and they want to cut down their dog-walking hours, they are taking on a full-time dog walker to help them.

David and Helen earn approximately £2,000 a week from their petsitting business during the winter and £3,000 a week in the summer. They also earn an income from their other pet services.

You can see why it's very hard to give you an exact figure because it depends on the time you've got available to work and how long it takes you to build up a regular customer base.

When I started out, over 12 years ago, I earned just £35 a week for the first three months. But I didn't have this book to help me!

Also, of course, the concept of petsitting is now far more widely known and the number of people using dog walkers and petsitters has risen dramatically since my early days.

Drawing up your petsitting business plan

If you can draw up a business plan, it can be a useful way of setting out what you hope to achieve in a certain time frame. When you look back at it, you will see if you have reached those milestones or goals you set yourself. Plans can also be crucial if you want to borrow money from your bank as they will like to see if you have a clear vision of your business future.

A basic plan might cover:

☐ A summary of what your business will offer e.g.: *Pete's Petsitting will be offering dog walking and pop in visits for pets.*

☐ Your qualifications and any experience.

☐ Who your competitors are, how much they charge and how they operate.

☐ A description of exactly what you will be offering e.g.: *I will be offering a dedicated dog-walking service for owners who cannot walk their dogs due to work or other time commitments.*

Pop in pet visits will involve visiting pet owners' homes while they are away, to feed and generally care for their pets, the majority of which will be cats.

For this work, I will be taking out specialist petsitter insurance to cover me for third-party liability to cover my business.

☐ Market research

Show that there is a demand for your service. Do any research yourself as market research companies are usually quite expensive. By following the guidelines in Chapter 2, Researching your market, you should be able to quote some figures.

☐ Legal matters

State that you will be a sole trader and that you have or will be informing the Inland Revenue and National Insurance office of your sole-trader status.

☐ Your objectives

Put down your goals for your petsitting business over the next 12 months. These should include how many clients you hope to have on your books and what kind of income you hope to have achieved by the end of your first year.

☐ Financial

If you are hoping to borrow money, then provide reasons why you need to. For example, you want to buy a van and equip it with integral cages.

Stick a copy of your business plan above your computer to refer to and to keep you on track!

❛ *It could only happen to a petsitter...*

A petsitter called Jes from New York was looking after two birds, an African grey and a cockatoo. She was looking out of the window to the other side of the street when she saw a green Amazon parrot sitting outside a window ledge.

Throwing on her coat, she went outside to try to save the parrot. She climbed up the stairs of one building, setting off the roof alarm before realizing that she's climbed up onto the wrong roof. A man shouted to her that people are only allowed on the roof in an emergency and that a bird isn't an emergency. She replied that if it was his bird, he would consider it an emergency.

She then rushed over two more buildings, climbed up onto another roof, looked over the side and there was the bird! Rushing down a ladder leading to the fire escape, she finally reached the bird...which turned out to be made of stone! ❜

2
RESEARCHING YOUR MARKET

In this chapter:

- ☐ Finding out whether there is a need in your area for a petsitting service
- ☐ Do you need to be licensed?
- ☐ Do you have to be police-checked?
- ☐ Joining a petsitting association
- ☐ Finding business start-up help
- ☐ Taking out specialist petsitter insurance.

Take a walk round your neighbourhood. How many pets do you think might live within walking distance of your home? According to PFMA, the Pet Food Manufacturers Association, one out every two households owns a pet, with cats now overtaking dogs in the popularity stakes.

This is how the latest statistics stand:

- ☐ 6.1 million cat-owning households
- ☐ 5.2 million dog-owning households
- ☐ 4.1 million fish-owning households
- ☐ 1.96 million rodent-owning households
- ☐ 1.39 million bird-owning households.

(source: PFMA, www.pfma.org.uk/overall /pet-population-figures-2.htm)

Finding out whether there is a need for a petsitting service in your area

Pet Plan, a well known pet insurer, states that:

> *New research reveals over two thirds of pet owners (69%) worry themselves sick about their pets when they head off on holidays. 27% make at least one call home to check in on their furry friends' welfare and a quarter (25%) consider their pet when making holidaying decisions. One Brit in ten will always take their pet on holiday with them and an extreme 6% of those who don't, worry enough to call home every day when holidaying.*

So even if there are already a number of petsitters established in your area, I think you'll find there is a real need for more.

If you want to do more research, try making up some questionnaires for pet owners and asking your local vets if you can leave them in their waiting rooms. A colleague of mine did this and, after describing herself and her reason for wanting to work with pets, asked the following questions:

- ☐ What pets do you have?

- ☐ What arrangements do you make for them when you are away?

- ☐ Would you consider using a petsitter or dog walker?

- ☐ Would you like a free assessment from a petsitter?

- ☐ Please state if you would like more information from me.

She was flooded with positive responses and is now becoming overwhelmed with clients and hoping that more petsitters will set up near her to take the pressure off.

Do you need to be licensed?

More and more local councils are insisting that anyone who boards dogs, not just kennel owners, must apply to them for a licence to do so. If you are thinking of offering a 'home from home' dog boarding service, check with your local council first.

If you want to set up as a dog walker, you should also contact your council if you need to be licensed by them to do this. Some councils, such as Wandsworth in London, for instance, specify the maximum number of dogs a professional dog walker may walk at any one time. When you call the council ask to speak to the licensing team for petsitters and dog walkers. This is still a fairly new area for them and you might otherwise spend ages explaining what a petsitter does.

Do you have to be police-checked?

You don't have to be but I think it's definitely worth doing because, in addition to your excellent references, it helps to reassure people that you have no criminal convictions.

Police checks are how many people refer to the process of subject data access. Unlike the more in-depth police background checks, the subject data access only checks to see if there are any criminal convictions in your name. It is limited, however, to the area you've lived in for the past year. Therefore if you have recently moved from London to Plymouth, for example, you should apply to both authorities to prove that you haven't been convicted of a crime in either county.

You can apply for a police check yourself. Find out who your local police authority is and request a Data Subject Access form. You can do this more quickly on the internet by going to the website of your local police authority, enter subject 'data access' in the search panel and download the form there. Or go to: www.met.police.uk/dataprotection. If you don't have internet access, write to:

National Identification Service
Subject Access Office
Room 350
New Scotland Yard
Broadway
London
SW1H 0BG

At the date of this publication, the current fee for carrying out a subject data access is £10. You will be asked to give the name of a professional person who can verify that as far as they are aware, you have lived at the same address for a certain number of years. You can then re-apply every year or so, in order to have an up-to-date letter to show your clients.

Joining a petsitting association

An association can be a good place to meet other petsitters and to keep up to date with changes in the profession. There are no petsitting unions as petsitters are, by and large, self-employed. If you want to join an association, then Pet Sitters International (www.petsit.com) is the largest petsitting association in the world. It has more than 8,000 members worldwide and although based in the USA, it is worth joining for its commitment to petsitters and their clients.

The *Petsitting News* (www.thepetsitting-news.com) has an online forum and chat room where petsitters can exchange information and offer help and support to each other.

Finding business start-up help

Petsitting is one of the few businesses where it really is possible to start up on a shoestring. You will, however, need to pay for petsitter insurance and there are some other costs you may need to consider. You may need to invest in a new laptop or PC. Your car might not have air conditioning, which is vital if you are transporting pets. Perhaps you are considering boarding pets and, if so, you might need new, secure fencing and other modifications to your property.

The Prince's Trust

If you are between 18 and 30, you are eligible to apply to the Prince's Trust, which a charity offering low cost loans and support.

Bank loans

Some banks have a set minimum amount of money they will lend. Don't be tempted to borrow more than you need. It will just take longer to pay back. Shop around for the lowest interest rates.

The Small Firms Loan Guarantee

This is a joint venture between the Department for Business, Enterprise and Regulatory Reform and a number of banks. It is especially useful for those without security to offer against a loan. It is worth asking your bank if they are participating in this scheme.

For more help with starting up a small business, find your local Business Link. Here you can obtain free advice and lots of information – www.businesslink.gov.uk.

Taking out specialist petsitter insurance

If you have pets of your own, you probably have them insured so you may wonder why more insurance is needed if your clients have also insured their pets. You need full public liability insurance. This is to cover you against any actions a person may take if you cause damage to them or their property. It is absolutely vital that you have this and your cover should be for a minimum of a million pounds. This only costs about £100 – £150 a year.

Here are some examples of why this insurance is absolutely essential.

Imagine you go into a client's house to feed their cats and knock over a hall table. On the table are a china figurine and a vase. They both smash to pieces on the tiled floor. These pieces may not be insured but your client is still eligible to claim damages from you, which could cost you hundreds of pounds.

Another vital insurance is key insurance. This is to cover you against locking yourself out and having to hire a locksmith to reach the pets inside. It will also cover you losing your clients' keys, which would result in them having to change their locks and keys before sending you a frighteningly large bill. Ask your insurance company if they will provide you with this cover.

Vehicle insurance. This can vary from company to company. You will need to inform your insurance provider that you are using your car or van for business. Explain how your vehicle is used – for example, transporting dogs to and from their homes and to parks or wherever you choose to walk them.

Here are a couple of companies who insure petsitters:

Cliverton
Tel: 01328 702010. www.cliverton.co.uk

Pet Business Insurance
Tel: 08450 220144. www.petbusinessinsurance.co.uk

Having insurance will give you and your clients peace of mind so it's worth every penny.

3
WHAT SERVICES CAN YOU OFFER?

In this chapter:

☐ Offering mobile pet care

☐ Dog walking

☐ Overnight petsitting or house sitting

☐ Home boarding

☐ Providing extra services.

For a petsitter, some typical clients might be a young professional couple with one dog. They leave for work early and come back around 7 p.m. They know that eight or nine hours is far too long to leave their dog without a loo break or exercise and they are also worried that she has started howling and tearing up their house. You could offer their dog a lunchtime walk or two shorter walks a day, depending on their budget and your schedule.

Other clients could be a retired couple who have a holiday planned. They have two elderly cats and don't want to leave them in a cattery because their cats hate any change in routine. Both cats are on medication. A pet pop-in service is ideal for them. The cats can stay in their own surroundings where they will be able to continue their medical treatment, be fed, groomed, cuddled and entertained.

Offering mobile pet care

Mobile pet care or pet pop-in services are how most petsitters describe a service where they visit a pet at home to feed it, clean any litter trays, hutches or cages and, most importantly, to spend time with the pet offering companionship and some TLC.

This is a great service for cats and other small animals and most petsitters will also bring in the post, open and close curtains and take other actions to give the house a 'lived in' appearance. This is ideal for owners who are on holiday. Fun, varied and always throwing up the unexpected, is how I would describe pop-in visits to care for pets staying in their own homes whilst their owners are at work or on holiday.

The most common request is for pop-in visits for cats. These are generally between half an hour to an hour, depending on the number of cats and whether they are indoor cats using a litter tray or have access to a garden through a cat flap.

Pet visits can usually be fitted around your more regular dog-walking times and/or if you are house sitting locally. They could also be included in the two or three hours you could reasonably be expected to be away from the house.

WHEN THE POP-IN SERVICE IS INAPPROPRIATE

Visits I rarely agree to are for dogs left at home alone in the house while the owners are on holiday. Dogs, being pack animals, don't care too much for their own company for such a long time. Being left alone for the day with a lunchtime walk with a petsitter, sleeping it off for a few hours and then greeting the owner around tea time is fine. However, a dog alone in his home day and night is not. The dog may howl and disturb the neighbours, chew the furniture, urinate everywhere and generally be unhappy.

The only exceptions I've made are when the dog is so elderly or infirm that to go into kennels really wouldn't be the best thing for him. The very best option is for his owners to hire a house sitter but sometimes this hasn't been possible and I have looked after such dogs. I have always insisted on the dog being visited between three and four times a day .

PERSONAL EXPERIENCE

A couple of years ago I agreed to visit and walk a dog called Teddy, who was a very old Collie aged 17. He was set in his ways and also quite unsociable. His owners had to leave him for a week because of family problems. Well, of course, I fell in love with him and he soon taught me that he liked his bed made a certain way, his food bowl to be put in the same place every day and which were his favourite walks. Being 17, he couldn't walk far so we'd spend the rest of the hour visit in his garden. I'd have a coffee and he would lie at my feet while I stroked him and we watched the world go by.

Dog walking

When I was petsitting full time, dog walking was the most requested service and one of the most fun to do. The petsitter collects the dog from the owner's house, walks it either alone or with other dogs, for anything between 20 minutes and an hour, depending on the service contract. The dog is then dropped back home again, hopefully tired and happy.

This is a cheaper option than all-day pet care or a dog crèche and is popular with petsitters because it's often an ongoing weekly booking, so they get the chance to really bond with the dog, enjoy its company, earn a regular fee – and get very fit!

Overnight petsitting or house sitting

This is really how the concept of petsitting started. The petsitter stays in the owner's home and cares for the pet while they're away.

Home sitting can be an ideal solution for anyone with a pet who is happier in their own environment, e.g. for an elderly or unsociable cat. For someone with two or more pets, this can often be more economical than paying multiple boarding fees to a kennel or cattery.

The owners also benefit by having their home lived in, as this greatly reduces the chances of being burgled. A barking dog is almost as good a deterrent as an alarm – although having both is better!

KNOWING WHAT TO EXPECT AS A HOUSE SITTER

As a house sitter, you are generally expected not to leave the home for longer than three or fours hours in 24. Some food may be provided for you, with a daily allowance for you to buy more. Alternatively you may be expected to pay for your food out of your fee depending on what you have agreed with the client and in your contract and terms and conditions.

If you are booked as a couple, only one of you will normally receive an allowance or the petsitting fee. You should ask if you are allowed to have guests to visit. Normally most clients are happy for you to have one friend over for lunch or dinner. Remember you will need this in writing and you will be responsible for your friend. In other words, if anything goes missing, you'll be liable.

If you are offered use of the owner's car, you must also have this in writing and make sure that you are insured to drive it.

Don't drink on duty. If you have a glass of wine, make sure it's from your own supply. I know this sounds really mean but even if your client has kindly said you can help yourself, it is unprofessional to do so. However, there is a far more important reason. You must stay within the legal driving limits at all times. A dog suffering from bloat, a horse who has cut herself on barbed wire at midnight or a cat who has managed to find a nice rat that's been feasting on Warfarin (rat poison) – these are all emergencies and, apart from the horse, you will have to get them to the vet urgently. And when the vet arrives to attend to the horse, she won't be very happy if you're three sheets to the wind and unable to assist with holding the horse's head during examination.

The house sitter should care for any pets as they would normally be cared for by their owners. Their meal times and exercise times should remain as close as possible to their usual routine. If the dog usually sleeps on the bed then you should let it sleep on the bed too. I know some petsitters would disagree with me on this but I don't think you should take the job if you aren't prepared to make the pets feel as secure and happy as possible. Obviously if the owner expects you to feed live mice to the python, you would probably decline the job – unless they would accept that you would be happier feeding the python dead mice instead.

As a house sitter, it is not part of your job to do housework or gardening other than to keep the house as clean and tidy as you found it. I usually try to make sure it is a little tidier than I found it but I don't overdo it. That can imply that your standards are higher than theirs (which they might be!). However, you are there to give them peace of mind, security and to build a good relationship with them, and having the owners feel that they have to leave an immaculate house rather than a comfortably tidy one is stressful for them. You will have already decided, during your initial consultation (see Chapter 8), if you are happy to stay in their home so there shouldn't be any surprises when you arrive.

DECIDING TO CONCENTRATE ON HOUSESITTING

If you decide to concentrate on house sitting, you should pick your clients carefully so that you aren't thrown in at the deep end. A family who leave you in charge of a large country house with three dogs, a horse and some free-range chickens for a month would be a lovely assignment but only after you have a good deal of experience in caring for those types of animals.

To offer house sitting, you will definitely need to show potential clients your 'police checked' letter and, even better, that you have been CRB cleared within the last 12 months. Being police checked is a reference to having applied to the police for any information about you which they might hold in the person record category of the Police National Computer. This is covered in Chapter 2.

CASE STUDY

Tricia Maw, a very experienced petsitter has found house sitting to be the perfect place to write some of her many published short stories. In an article she wrote about house sitting, Tricia states: *'The work is varied. I've looked after many different animals, from a Rhodesian Ridgeback to a Yorkshire Terrier, from ordinary moggies to aristocratic Siamese, from an African Grey parrot (who talked non-stop) to a tankful of tropical fish and a rather large iguana.*

Living in other people's houses is a strange experience at first but you very quickly get used to a new environment. I've stayed in suburban bungalows and Grade 11 listed houses, I've watered house plants and made tea for the gardener and I've loved every minute of it!

And, best of all, none of my charges have ever answered me back – apart from the parrot!'

Home boarding

Offering a home-from-home boarding service for pets has become one of the fastest growth areas of petsitting in the UK and the biggest users of this service are dog owners.

It's easy to see the attraction for pet owners. There's no worrying about letting virtual strangers into their home and last-minute bookings are usually easier to arrange because so many petsitters offer home boarding.

I did a lot of home boarding when I first started up. From what I've learned and observed over the years, I can offer the following heartfelt advice. Please don't even consider home boarding if you have children, pets of your own, live near a busy main road or don't have suitable premises. Ask yourself: 'is my partner going to be fine with this too?' Unless you live alone, whoever lives with you is going to be involved whether they like it or not.

Equally important to ask yourself is whether you have the knowledge, aptitude and experience to do this. Boarding dogs is a different situation altogether compared to dog walking or pet visiting. The risk factor is higher for both the boarded dog and you. I say this after hearing so many stories of lost dogs and accidents. Here's just a sample:

☐ A petsitter employed a tradesman to work at her house and the tradesmen left a door open, allowing the dog to escape.

☐ A boarded dog attacked the petsitter's cat.

☐ A petsitter's dogs attacked the boarded dog.

☐ A dog badly cut his paw, which the petsitter wrapped in a dirty cloth and left. By the time the owners collected the dog, he needed emergency treatment to save his leg.

☐ A boarded puppy found and ate the petsitter's painkillers, resulting in severe kidney problems for the poor puppy.

☐ A boarded dog attacked another dog out on a walk while being boarded with a petsitter. The injured dog had to be put to sleep.

Any of the above could have happened to me. I was the worst petsitter – well, almost, I have met worse – when I started off all those years ago, because I knew nothing about petsitting and I made so many mistakes. Of course, I thought it would be a piece of cake. I knew loads about dogs and loved being with them, so how hard could it be?

There were no books, guidelines or petsitting colleagues when I started. I thought that because the two dogs I walked got on beautifully together with my dog out in the woods, they would get on beautifully together in my house when both their owners decided to go on holiday at the same time.

I had one male dog of my own, Archie and I boarded a whippet called Jo and a golden retriever called Bobby. On the fourth day – and it is usually the third or fourth day that a dominant dog will assert himself and challenge the lead dog – Bobby had a fight with my dog. We had to separate them into different rooms and take them out at different times. (By the way, I've changed the names here to protect the innocent – or not so innocent). Then Archie decided that he didn't like Jo, the whippet, any more so there was more allocating of rooms, gardens and walks. By the time Bobby and Jo's owners came back, my husband and children weren't speaking to me.

So don't be fooled into thinking that just because your dog walks happily with another dog, they will get on well together under one roof. A dog's behaviour and what he will and won't accept from another dog can change dramatically if the dog enters his home.

In addition to the government's regulations concerning home boarding, my criteria for boarding dogs would include:

☐ No children under 16 to be living in your home or to visit you while you have a dog to stay.

☐ No pets of your own unless you are an APBC pet behaviour counsellor who would almost certainly know the dog they were boarding, its personality and idiosyncrasies.

☐ Only one dog boarding at any one time.

☐ You should have a secure home – each exit should have a double door system and dog gates.

☐ Your garden should have six-foot secure fencing with a double lockable gate.

☐ Your house shouldn't be next to a busy main road.

☐ No dog should be left alone in the house for more than four hours in 24.

☐ No dog should be crated at any time, no matter what the owners do at home.

☐ Only in emergencies should there be any cross-over between one client's dog and the next.

LOOKING AT HOME BOARDING FROM THE DOG'S POINT OF VIEW

You need to have a good understanding of canine behaviour, and I don't just mean that you've had a few dogs of your own and think you know enough about canine behaviour.

Let's say your dog, we'll call him Max, has found his level in your household. He knows where he's allowed to sit, which rooms are out of bounds. He is at one in his dog world within your human world – and then comes the unwanted visitor. Suddenly Max's territory has been invaded and he has to adjust. At best, the boarded dog will be a female and, even better, she will be his size or smaller. This might mean he doesn't object quite so much – in fact he quite likes her as long as she doesn't go near his food bowl or jump on your lap. Perhaps, though, the guest is a large dominant male dog. Let's call him Dan. You've had him to stay for a trial weekend and he's been good as gold. In reality, though, he's spent the weekend sizing up the status quo and has discovered that your dog is fairly submissive. By the third day, he makes it quite clear to your dog, Max, that he, Dan, the guest dog, is now in charge. He might do this quite subtly and Max may accept it.

The worst-case scenario is that Dan goes for Max or that Max refuses to accept Dan's claim to top dog and you have a the recipe for trouble.

You can imagine the stress levels of a dog who is left in a house with people he doesn't know and worse, a dog or two who he also doesn't know and who may well view him as a threat. People he can get used to, if they are kind and treat him well, but other dogs are a different matter. He would, I think, be much happier in a good kennel in a completely safe environment with his own space around him.

So along with all the variables – dog bites child, workman leaves back gate open, child 'strokes' dog too hard, dog eats pet rabbit, cat scratches dog – you have to think about the psychological effects that an unsuitable environment has on a dog.

Don't give in to emotional blackmail when people call you to say that if you can't have their dog to stay, it will have to go in a kennel. What's wrong with that? There are some fantastic kennels out there – I've listed some in the back of this book. There are also some dire ones, but there are some dire petsitters as well.

Tell the owner to get in touch with the recently formed British Kennels and Catteries Association, BKCA, for a list of kennels registered with them. The Pet Care Trust has all the relevant information about BKCA, on their website, www.petcare.org.uk.

If you don't have children under 16, or pets of your own, and you do have a good sized house in a quiet neighbourhood with a secure garden and the knowledge and experience plus pet first aid training, then you could be an excellent host for canine guests.

Some petsitters also offer day boarding, where the dog's owners drop their dog off at the petsitter's house before going to work and pick it up again on the way home – a bit like childminding. This service is also subject to regulations and, again, your local council can advise you on this. For more information about the full legal requirements of home boarding, see Chapter 4, 'Legal, health and safety'.

I don't know anyone who home-boards cats and I wouldn't recommend it. Cats are much happier staying in their own environment with either a house sitter or with visits from a petsitter. There are also many excellent catteries up and down the country.

Providing extra services

DOG CRÈCHE

This is a concept which has been popular in America for a while and is starting to catch on in the UK. A dog crèche is run on similar lines to a crèche for babies and pre-school age children. Dog owners drop their dogs off at the crèche before going to work and pick them up again when they return. The dogs usually spend their day in a large play room with access to an outdoor area and individual inside kennels.

Unlike other types of petsitting, a dog crèche requires substantial investment and is subject to stricter regulations.

PUPPY VISITS

These are very similar to other pet visits but puppies have very special requirements and will generally need more time and care spent on them. You will need to have a good knowledge of puppy development and need to offer top-quality care so prepare before you advertise in this area of pet care by reading Gwen Bailey's *How to Have a Perfect Puppy*.

Puppy pop-ins sound very appealing, and who could resist spending time with a cute bundle of fun, but they can be quite demanding. If the puppy is alone from the time the owners leave at say, 8 a.m. to their return at 6 p.m. – that's a long day. Depending on the puppy's age, it should be visited every couple of hours when it is very young to every four hours as it grows. There is more information on this in Chapter 10, 'How to care for home-alone pets'.

Microchipping, grooming, dog training and pet behaviour are also services that some petsitters, once they are trained and qualified, have added to their portfolio.

❛ It could only happen to a petsitter…

While house sitting at a beautiful home for clients who were away in another country for a month, a petsitter decided that it seemed a shame not to make full use of the owners' swimming pool on the lawn. She invited about 20 friends around and they enjoyed a hot June day, jumping in and out of the pool and eating and drinking al fresco with a huge barbeque. All that spoiled an otherwise perfect day was an irritating little aeroplane buzzing low in the sky.

A few weeks after the assignment finished, the petsitter was very surprised when the clients turned up at her house, in somewhat of a temper. They handed the petsitter a large photograph. With horror, she saw that it was an aerial photograph of the owners' house and garden complete with a hoard of inebriated revellers swimming in their pool and cooking on their barbeque. All snapped up by a photographer on that annoying little aeroplane. ❜

4
LEGAL, HEALTH AND SAFETY

In this chapter:

- ☐ Animal Welfare Act 2006

- ☐ Data Protection Act 1988

- ☐ Trade Descriptions Act 1968

- ☐ Health and Safety at Work Act 1974

- ☐ Animal Boarding Establishments Act 1963.

I know it's tempting to jump in and start petsitting but you will first need a working knowledge of any legislation that may apply to you. There are many excellent books that cover, in detail, how to set up a small business and although this book is intended to help you with the petsitting side of the business, you might also like to read *Make it your Business*, which is a very helpful book for anyone starting out in business.

Feel free to skip this chapter for now but please do read it before you set up. Once you are up and running, you may be too busy. I found a good time to study the information here was the time between advertising for clients and receiving my first enquiry. You may find, however, that the moment you start advertising, you start getting enquiries, so why don't you grab a coffee and we'll go through the 'must know' stuff?

Animal Welfare Act 2006

This is the first amended Animal Welfare Act (AWA) for nearly a hundred years and not only does it set higher standards in animal welfare, it will make our jobs as petsitters easier too.

Since the 1911 Animal Welfare Act, not only has the way we lived changed tremendously but also our attitude to animals. Our knowledge of how animals think, feel and suffer has increased hugely over the last century. We now understand that we are responsible not only for their physical welfare but for their psychological welfare too.

In the past, should you have seen an obviously malnourished, neglected horse in a field, unless that horse was lying down, then not you or even the RSPCA could enter that field to examine the animal without the owner's permission.

In the early part of the last century, it was widely believed that animals were incapable of mental suffering and therefore the only legal requirement for an animal, such as a dog, was that he should have access to food, water and shelter.

This meant that a dog could be kept in an outside kennel or cooped up in a crate or small room, never walked, stroked or given soft bedding to lie on. A dog left to such a miserable existence for years on end obviously suffers and this suffering can result in severe behavioural problems. I use this as an example because one of the first dogs I ever walked was treated like this and it was only through the intervention of a caring veterinary nurse that I was given the wonderful job of opening his door to freedom.

The reasons why you should have a working knowledge of this Act, amongst other laws, is so you can use it to help you in many aspects of your business. The most obvious is that you will know what kind of conditions are acceptable for an owner to keep their pet in and what standards must be met.

I used my knowledge of the law as it applies to pets, to set a baseline for my terms and conditions and my pet service contracts. I have my own standards which are, in some cases, higher than those required by the AWA but it is useful to quote this Act in my paperwork so that owners who may be unaware that such legislation even exists, are under no illusion that I know my stuff.

The new law makes owners and keepers responsible for ensuring that the welfare needs of their animals are met. I think these sections of the Act are worth learning by heart.

Responsibility for animals.

For the purposes of this Act, a person shall be treated as responsible for any animal for which a person under the age of 16 years of whom he has actual care and control is responsible.

Duty of Care (s9)

A person commits an offence if he does not take such steps as are reasonable in all the circumstances to ensure that the needs of an animal for which he is responsible are met to the extent required by good practice.

For the purposes of this Act, an animal's needs shall be taken to include:

(a)   its need for a suitable environment,
(b)   its need for a suitable diet,
(c)   its need to be able to exhibit normal behaviour patterns,
(d)   any need it has to be housed with, or apart from, other animals, and
(e)   its need to be protected from pain, suffering, injury and disease.

This is a very brief summary of the Animal Welfare Act as I believe it applies to pet owners and petsitters.

☐ Pet owners have a duty of care to make sure that the welfare needs of their pets are met.

☐ Pet owners must provide a standard of care that meets certain criteria for that type of animal's welfare.

☐ The owner must provide a suitable environment and living quarters for their pets. The pet must have enough room, a warm and comfortable sleeping area, adequate shelter and be in a clean and safe environment. A rabbit, for instance, should be able to stand upright on its hind quarters and have a hutch at least six times larger than itself. Attached should be a predator-proofed run.

☐ The pet owner must provide a suitable diet with constant access to fresh water.

☐ The pet must be housed with, or apart from, other animals if this is applicable. For example, Syrian hamsters should be kept alone because they will fight to the death, whereas rabbits should always be kept in pairs and may become depressed if not.

☐ The pet owner must protect the pet from pain, injury, suffering and disease.

☐ The pet owner must protect the animal from fear and distress and protect it from mental suffering. A dog kept in a kitchen for 24 hours a day and never walked, will, in my opinion, be in mental distress.

Anyone found guilty of cruelty to an animal or who doesn't provide for its welfare needs can be fined up to £20,000 and/or sent to prison. A ban on owning animals can also be made. Owners can be prosecuted if these needs are not met. These include parents of children who 'own' animals.

To read this or any Acts of Parliament in full, visit www.opsi.gov.uk/acts.htm.

Data Protection Act 1988

You are the 'data controller' of your business and if you keep information about your clients on your computer or as hard copy, you need to be aware of how the Data Protection Act applies to you.

Anyone who you collect data about – your clients – should be told the following.

(a)   You are keeping this information about them as a record in your files or on your computer. They will obviously expect you to do this anyway but you should reassure them that any such information will be kept in a locked filing cabinet.

(b)   The data will only be seen by you and your staff and won't be used for any other purpose other than to help you care for their pets and homes.

(c)   The information will be destroyed if irrelevant or if they no longer require your services, and will not be sold or given away.

Be aware: I have heard of petsitters being scammed by companies trying to charge them to add them to the Data Protection Register. If you are contacted in this way, contact your local trading standards office.

Protecting your clients' details under the Data Protection Act needn't be complicated (see Chapter 14, 'Running your home office').

The Information Commissioner's website, www.ico.gov.uk, has lots of help and information, as does www.smallbusiness.co.uk.

Trade Descriptions Act 1968

The purpose of this Act is to make sure no one advertises goods and services inaccurately. If you are selling something or offering a service in return for payment, your business advertising and marketing must accurately reflect what is being sold.

For example, if an inexperienced petsitter advertises that she has been police checked, has a certificate in pet first aid and is recommended by her local vet, and she has none or only one or two of these qualities, then, in my opinion and probably in a potential client's opinion, she is violating the Trade Descriptions Act. Only Trading Standards could prosecute her but if she failed in her duty of care and a pet she was caring for had an accident, then her insurance company – if she was insured, that is – would look dimly on her claim for compensation should the owners sue her.

Health and Safety at Work Act 1974

This really only applies if you have staff for whom you are responsible for their safety, but I think it is well worth studying to find out how you can make your own working environment as safe as possible. If, for example, you are meeting a client in their home to discuss pet care visits in their absence, a good knowledge of the Health and Safety Act will highlight any hazardous aspects of the home and conditions you will be working in. You should, for instance, always have access to two exits from the home in case one is blocked by fire or flood. To read the full act, go to: www.direct.gov.uk/en/Employment/Employees/HealthAndSafetyAtWork/.

I've summarized the points I think are most relevant for petsitters.

☐ The temperature you're working in should be comfortable. Around 16°C for 'sedentary' workplace (e.g. caring for a cat in its owner's home).

☐ There should be enough light for you to move around and work in safely.

☐ The workplace and equipment should be clean. (If you visited a home which was reasonably clean and then found it filthy when you did your first pet care visit, I would quote this to the owners.)

☐ The area you work in should be properly ventilated.

☐ All windows, doors and gates should be easy to open, with safety devices if needed.

☐ '…employees who work alone, or off-site, can do so safely and healthily'. (If you visit a house and feel you might not be safe or you are asked to walk a dog in an unsafe environment, then refuse. The law's on your side.)

These are all things to look out for when you do your initial client consultations (see Chapter 8).

Animal Boarding Establishments Act 1963

> *References in this Act to the keeping by any person of a boarding establishment for animals shall, subject to the following provisions of this section, be construed as references to the carrying on by him at premises of any nature (including a private dwelling) of a business of providing accommodation for other people's animals.*
>
> *(www.opsi.gov.uk/acts)*

My interpretation of this Act is that if you board pets, as a business, from your own home, you need to be licensed to do so. I can't think of any good reason why a petsitter wouldn't want to be licensed. I wouldn't want to leave my pets anywhere that hadn't been inspected by a council animal welfare officer or vet.

In Chapter 3, 'What services can you offer?', I discussed how experienced and knowledgeable you needed to be to offer home boarding and how thorough you'd have to be to ensure the well-being and health of pets you boarded. So many factors – your family, your home and any resident pets – would have to be considered.

Councils, who license petsitters to home board pets, use this Act as a basis for the conditions of the licence. Not all councils license home boarding but you should double-check by ringing your local council and ask to speak to someone on the licensing team. You may find that they have had a lot of experience with licensing home boarders; or they might not even have come across a petsitter who wants to do this in their area. Even if you are the first one, once you explain the service you want to offer, they will probably insist that you are visited by an animal welfare officer and that he is happy with the environment the pets would be kept in.

I understand this to mean that irrespective of whether or not your council currently offers licence applications for home boarders, if you take money for boarding pets in your own home, you need to register in some way with your council.

Don't be put off contacting your council just because you know that the petsitter down the road hasn't registered or if you believe your council doesn't require you to register with them. I know it's another expense but it's a small one – between £40 and £80 seems to be the average cost – and you will be so much better protected and will have more information to offer much better boarding than the petsitter down the road.

Below is just a brief summary of some of the conditions laid down by council licensing teams. Often there are over 70 conditions stipulated in the conditions of granting a licence.

☐ The council will certainly want to see that any construction (i.e. your home) is suitable, with no dogs being crated or kennelled but living as part of the family.

☐ You should limit your number of boarded dogs (normally to one at a time) and that you don't board dogs with resident cats unless they live with a cat at home (still dodgy in my opinion).

☐ You won't be allowed to board dogs registered under the Dangerous Wild Animal Act, e.g. wolf hybrids.

☐ Obviously bitches in season can't be boarded with resident dogs. Nor puppies under the age of six months.

☐ You'll need to know how to isolate dogs in cases of contagious disease outbreaks and to take all precautions against parasite infestation.

☐ A register will be required of all dogs boarded.

☐ Fire and emergency precautions must be taken.

☐ Training and supervision of employees and helpers must be carried out.

☐ Dogs should be exercised in accordance with owners' instructions.

☐ Cleanliness is always paramount and you'll need to agree disposal facilities for pet waste with the council.

If your own council doesn't have a licence application form you can download or request, then study some other councils' forms. One source is: www.charnwood.gov.uk/environment/animalboarding.html.

5
GETTING YOUR BUSINESS STARTED

In this chapter:

- ☐ Assembling the tools of the trade

- ☐ Shopping list for petsitting supplies

- ☐ Establishing your client area

- ☐ Setting your prices

- ☐ Your vehicle

- ☐ Determining your policy

- ☐ Naming your business.

Assembling the tools of the trade

You will need both office and petsitting 'tools' to run your business so let's start with some basic office supplies.

- ☐ PC or laptop

- ☐ Telephone

- ☐ Large desk diary/Filofax

- ☐ Small diary/Filofax, for when you're on the move

- ☐ Filing cabinet

- ☐ Index box file with cards

- ☐ A5 plastic envelopes

- ☐ Small-change bags

- ☐ A4 size plastic folders either zip-up or snap-shut for full client records

- ☐ Accounts book

- ☐ Diary and work planner

- ☐ Large pin board

☐ Spare key tags

☐ Stationery/pens/stamps

☐ Book case

☐ Business cards

☐ Local area maps

☐ Footpath maps if you're going to be dog walking

☐ Shredder

☐ Tote bag or other large bag to hold daily petsitting tools and paperwork

☐ Desk or table.

PC OR LAPTOP (AND A PRINTER)

You can run a business without one but it's much easier if you do have one. You can communicate with your clients easily, build a website and design and print off most of your business stationery from business cards, brochures, contracts to newsletters for your clients.

Over time, I found that I was happiest using both my computer and hard-copy paper filing to run my home office. Computers are brilliant but they can crash and if you haven't backed up your work or you rely solely on your website or email for taking bookings, then you're at the mercy of a computer engineer or your web server. And…'Sod's Law' dictates that computers will always crash in your busiest season.

TELEPHONE

Don't use your home phone number for business without informing your phone company as they may have a policy on using a residential line for business.

You could have one phone and have a separate number for your petsitting business. There are a few ways you can do this: BT provides a service where calls to your business number are forwarded to your landline and/or mobile. If your phone number isn't easy for clients to remember, then this is worth considering. You can buy an 0845 number for around 50 pounds. You could also think about buying a 'no frills' mobile phone and use this as your business phone.

 Smile when you record your answer phone message. Yes, it really does make a difference. If you want callers to call you on a different number, dictate the number very slowly. I wish I could give this advice to potential clients too. Many times I've had to play back an answerphone message to try and make out a rushed or garbled contact.

LARGE DESK DIARY

I use an A4 size Filofax, which has lots of useful pockets, zips and notepaper. When a client phones, instead of scribbling their name and number on a scrap of paper (always get this information before entering into a conversation), put it down in that day's entry. You then have a permanent record of the day the client contacted you, their contact details and you will have your diary open, ready to check dates.

FILING CABINET (WITH AT LEAST THREE DRAWERS)

The whole cabinet must be lockable if you intend retaining owners' keys for them. This will be one of your most vital pieces of equipment, if not the most exciting. You need a three-drawer one so that you can dedicate one drawer to customer keys, which must stay in a secure and locked place when not in use. Client details should also be under lock and key to conform to the Data Protection Act (see Chapter 4).

INDEX BOX FILE WITH CARDS

These are your biggest allies in keeping manageable records of your potential and existing clients. When you buy your index box, buy double the amount of cards to go in the boxes. Every time you have a firm booking, copy all the relevant information from your client information sheet on to one card. On the second card copy information most useful for your visit but don't copy the owner's name or address or anything which would identify their property if the card got into the wrong hands.

The first card with the owner's address will be kept permanently in your storage box. The second card will be kept in your filing cabinet inside the client's folder when not in use.

A5 PLASTIC ENVELOPES

You can buy these from most stationers or, as I do, from eBay. If you put your second box card (the one without the client's name and address) in one of these it can be kept with you throughout the pet care visit. If you pop the client's keys in here too, then you know where they are at all times.

SMALL-CHANGE BAGS

Use bank small change bags to put the client's keys into first as sometimes the sharp key edges gradually tear the envelopes. Alternatively, wear the keys around your neck on a piece of leather or chain, around your wrist or attached to your belt.

PLASTIC FOLDERS – A4 SIZE

These are ideal for keeping the client's file in and also for leaving with the client at each visit or permanently, if you visit regularly. I like to leave a log of my visits with a copy for myself plus a copy of all the information I might need about that particular pet. This means the client can always check to see if they need to update me with anything relating to their pet. It may become diabetic, for example, or the house alarm code could be changed or emergency contact details might need updating.

ACCOUNTS BOOK

Even if you use accounting software such as QuickBooks (www.QuickBooks.co.uk) or Sage (www.sage.co.uk), having a paper record is a good back-up and its easier to use if, for instance, you want to jot down that you have just spent £12.00 on a pet care book. Buy the best software you can afford, as you will be using it either daily or weekly to enter your income and expenditure.

DIARY AND WORK PLANNER

A large desk diary and a pocket diary are ideal – a Blackberry is even better but we're trying to keep your start up cost as low as possible remember, no harm putting one on your wish list though.

LARGE PIN BOARD

Get the biggest you can fit on your wall. This, for me, is one of the most useful items. Mine is covered with articles from pet magazines, the latest leaflets from my vet concerning, for example, new vaccinations against kennel cough, precautions to take against avian flu and foot and mouth. My weekly schedule is up there so I can see at a glance where I should be at any given time or day. I pin up 'return calls', to-do lists – in fact, anything which I want to be reminded of as soon as I walk into the room or need to have at my fingertips.

BOOK CASE OR BOOKSHELVES

You will probably have an ever-growing collection of pet care books and you'll need to refer to them and keep yourself up to date with advances in the treatment and welfare of pets. If you are asked to care for gerbils, then a quick trip to the library, bookshop or internet will provide you with a reference book. With this you can at least gain some basic knowledge before visiting the owner and their gerbils.

BUSINESS CARDS

These are easy to make yourself or you can get them printed for a very low cost, sometimes free, from www.vistaprint.com. You can also have them printed professionally from a local printer.

LOCAL AREA MAPS

You can always Google a client's address but having local maps on you and/or in you car is really helpful. If you intend to offer a dog walking service get yourself a pathfinder map. I have got lost so many times when dog walking, even in areas I thought I knew. True, I do have a lousy sense of direction but taking a wrong turn in a forest where all the paths look the same can lead you miles out of your way. Having a road map on your wall means you can see at a glance if an owner is too far away for you. You can also plan your route if you need to.

A DESK OR TABLE (AND THE COMFIEST OFFICE CHAIR YOU CAN GET)

A room of your of your own is ideal but not everyone has the luxury of a spare room. If you do and it's currently housing your boyfriend's collection of seventies heavy metal albums or your now teenager children once used it as a playroom, then claim it and don't use it for anything but your business. That means it can't be used as a dumping ground for ironing or for mending bikes. It is your office now.

If you don't have a room of your own, you'll manage fine with a kitchen table or by putting a desk in your bedroom. The only problem I had with this was that my sons would dump their school bags down on my desk and when I moved the desk to our bedroom my husband would use it too. You have to be firm.

Your desk diary, pet forms and note pads will take up at least a third of a large kitchen table, if not all of it. If you use the table at meal times, try to have a small desk or even some box files where you can quickly store your things. I'm typing this in my kitchen with a Jack Russell on my lap and a cat on the table. The cat, Mo, is watching a bird in the garden and any moment now, she's going to walk across the laptop. For me, it still beats working in a real office job, though.

Shopping List for Petsitting Supplies

GOOD BOOTS OR WATERPROOF TRAINERS (2 PAIRS)

They don't have to be expensive but they need to be waterproof, well cushioned and easy to take on and off when you enter clients' homes.

WATER PROOF TROUSERS

Nothing is worse than wet trousers that cling to your legs, making them wet and cold. Keep waterproof trousers rolled up in your car for when the heavens open.

WATER- OR SHOWERPROOF JACKETS

Unlike shopping, where you are strolling more than speed walking, you will get very warm quickly so having a heavy waxed coat or thick padded jacket is going to make you hot and uncomfortable; so layering is best. Get a couple of lightweight, waterproof jackets which cover your bottom and have lots of pockets – preferably zipped. Underneath you can have a t-shirt and/or a sweatshirt or sweater. If you wear a shirt over a t-shirt and a woollen scarf in winter and a thinner silk or cotton one in summer, you'll always have two of the most useful pet first aid items – see Chapter 13, 'Pet first aid'.

If you are going to include dog walking in your business, then try buying some clothes that can cope with the demands of your job and our temperamental English weather. Regatta, www.regatta.com, is a good choice as they sell well-designed trousers with multiple pockets. Some of their range is waterproof and has an SPF factor (sun protection factor). Sweatshirts and polo shirts are not only practical but can be personalized with your logo and website address.

DOG LEADS

Use the strongest and brightest you can find.

COLLARS AND TAGS

I prefer to use collars which have my mobile number embroidered on them, as name tags can get pulled off in bushes. If you do this, however, you need to give each dog you walk his collar, to limit the chances of spreading any infections.

TOWELS

Have a good supply of towels and, if possible, Vet Beds, which are densely woven pieces of synthetic sheepskin. These can be washed at 60 degrees and are very hardwearing and versatile. They can be used as pet beds, thrown over chairs and sofas to protect them and to offer a comfortable, cosy place for a tired dog or cat, and they are ideal for covering the hatch area of your car or as liners for dog crates. See Resources for suppliers.

PET FIRST AID KITS

Have a large pet first aid kit in your home office and a smaller one in your car or in your bum bag.

BUM BAG

A good-quality bum bag with pockets for your mobile phone, pet treats, money, snacks for you, spare leads and business cards.

A DOG CRATE

I never use these as cages but they can be a great sanctuary for a frightened or sick pet. Leave the door permanently open and cover three-quarters of the crate with a large blanket to make the perfect den for a shy dog. They are also perfect for the hatch of an estate car, jeep or van. By using two or three, if you can fit them in your vehicle, you won't have to worry about carrying multiple dogs in the back of your car.

INTERACTIVE PET TOYS

Kongs (available from the Company of Animals, www.companyofanimals.com), for cats, dogs and parrots are strong rubber cones, which you can stuff with a mixture of treats and either a ready-made Kong filler or peanut butter. These keep pets occupied for ages, which is really useful if they are left alone for long periods. They are also good for overweight pets as they satisfy a desire to chew with the extra reward of food. Chewing a Kong, like gnawing at a bone in the wild, uses up calories so it's a great tool in the fight against flab. If only there was one for humans!

POO BAGS

Buy these in bulk from a pet shop. Don't use supermarket carrier bags – they have air holes.

RAPE ALARM

Carry a lightweight rape alarm. Not only will this make you feel more secure, the piercing noise it makes can help break up a dogfight or scare off an aggressive pet.

DOG HARNESSES

I prefer not to use a traditional collar-and-lead arrangement when I walk dogs because even with a correctly fitted collar, with the temptation of another dog on the other side of a road or in a fearful situation a dog can wriggle out of it. Even with the more padded types of collars, there is also a danger of damage to the dog's thorax or throat; this is especially true of choke chains which is why I never use even half-chokes.

I've found the best harnesses are ones that can be used as a walking harness and as a safety restraint in the car. Dogs should never be harnessed in the front passenger seat if you have an airbag fitted as the pressure released can break a dog's ribs and possibly kill him. The same applies to the back seats if you have airbags there, in which case you will need a large hatchback or estate car.

WATER BOWLS

These should be light and dishwasher proof. Wash them daily. Keep plastic non-spill ones in the car, as water needs to be available to your pet clients, all year round, no matter how cold it is.

TORCHES

Keep one large torch for your car and a pen-size one for your bum bag.

CHOCOLATE

Always have some kind of high-sugar snack like chocolate or glucose tablets on you because if you get lost on a dog walk or stuck in your car for ages, you don't want low blood sugar to cause you problems. Chocolate is toxic to dogs and the higher the percentage of cocoa, the more dangerous it is, so ignore any begging looks and eat it yourself.

Establishing your client area

A common mistake some new petsitters make is trying to spread themselves too thinly. It's so easy to do. You get an enquiry from someone who lives 12 miles away. You've only just started and have just two regular clients. Think, though, of the time you'll spend travelling to and from this client, the petrol and wear and tear on your car. It may be hard to turn it down but if you don't have enough clients in that area to make it worth your while, I wouldn't accept the assignment. If you can pass it on to another petsitter, she may well do the same for you, so build a list of petsitters to whom you would be happy referring people to.

Whether you offer a visit of 20 minutes or an hour, that's how long you spend with the pet and doesn't include travelling to and from the client's house. You'll need to leave space between visits to give yourself enough time or you'll get exhausted rushing from one place to another. You'll start feeling guilty too if you are cutting down the length of a dog's outing or a cat's only chance for human company that day.

When I first started I decided that I would accept clients from within a ten-mile radius of home. My thinking was that while I was building up the business and wouldn't have many customers, beggars couldn't be choosers. Once I had a good base of local clients, I reasoned, I would pass them on to other dog walkers and petsitters and stick to my local area, which would be more profitable.

After six months of very little business, I suddenly had more clients than I could cope with. I couldn't keep to my plan of giving my out-of-town pets to my peers because they were thin on the ground and run off their feet as it was. Also, what I hadn't considered was how very fond of my long distance-dogs and cats – and rabbit – I would become. They all had little peculiarities which I had come to recognize and, where possible, accommodate. Jake, the dalmatian, was frightened of pushchairs and black dogs; Maisie, the yorkie, didn't like rain or strong winds; and the two German shepherd brothers were scared of all other dogs. Only Clive, the rabbit, seemed well balanced enough to cope with his life as best friend to a donkey. So I looked after these pets and with most of them, only just broke even on my fuel and time expenditure. Over the next couple of years, Clive's owner got a job where she didn't have to travel so didn't need me, Maisie's mum had a baby and she gave up work and stayed at home, Jake's owner moved to the north and the German shepherds died at the great ages of 14 and 15.

Once you are established, you will find that you can travel a little further to your clients because you will be visiting other pets who live near or on the way to your furthest client, making it worth your while.

Drive around your area. Time yourself and make a note of how much petrol you use and traffic conditions at different times of the day.

Don't be put off if you find there are already petsitters in your area. They may be as over-stretched as I was and be glad to pass clients your way. If they are a large petsitting company, they are probably charging top whack because they have to pay their dog walkers and pet carers at least the minimum wage. You will be another choice for pet owners. Not every petsitter gets on with every pet or client and owners may have stayed with someone they don't feel comfortable with because there is no one else. Study the competition. Is there anything you could offer or specialize in which they don't cover?

Setting your prices

Lots of petsitters have websites where they state their prices – although usually not a price for every service – that is more likely to be in their brochure or price list.

Don't call up companies pretending to be a prospective client wanting information and prices. I can always tell and sometimes they don't even think to block their phone numbers for 1471. If you email, your computer address is available too so just call them saying you are new to the area and are setting up in business and can they give you any advice. The majority of petsitters are helpful, kind and friendly and will go out of their way to help you. You are always going to get one or two who feel threatened and may try and put you off, but don't let them.

What do you think you are worth? How much do you want to earn an hour or a day? This is a more positive way to think about your earning potential than how much you think clients would pay or what another dog walker charges.

Keep it simple. Don't charge different rates for different people unless they have more than a set number of pets. We often have discussions or polls about pricing and other issues on the *Petsitting News* website, and these are an example of some petsitters fees in May 2008.

Dog walking	£10 per hour
One-to-one dog walking	£15 per half hour
Puppy visits	£15 per hour
Public holiday visits	Charged at double time
Rats, rabbits, guinea pigs, etc	£10 per visit
Cat care visits – up to 3 cats	£10 per visit

I know that looking after three cats who use litter trays is going to be harder work than caring for one cat who has free access to his garden and doesn't need a litter tray, but you are always going to get relatively easy assignments and more challenging ones and as long as this difference isn't going to take you well over your allotted time, I wouldn't tie yourself in knots quoting different rates and time scales.

Review your prices annually – April is a good time as that's when most people get a rise in line with inflation and it's far enough away from Christmas.

Always have 'Prices correct as of April 10th', for example, on your price list or brochure so that clients know that everyone is charged at the same rate and that you don't chop and change.

Understandably, when starting out, petsitters are often inclined to keep their fees low or undercut other petsitters.

Find out what other petsitters charge and try to keep your fees roughly in line with theirs. This is really not the kind of business where undercutting the competition is worthwhile unless it is a company who employs petsitters. As you are your own employer, your costs are lower so your prices should be able to reflect this. But because you are on your own or perhaps working with a partner, there will be times when you do get sick or have a family emergency you need to deal with. Rather than letting your customers down, by forming bonds with your peers, you can always ask one of them to cover for you. Having a contingency plan is a great idea as well (see Chapter 15).

It is easier to say than to do, but don't try and justify your charges or let potential clients try to beat you down. It happens now and then so be prepared. You can't tell what type of person is more likely to haggle with you, so practise saying something like: 'This is my rate for cat care visits but I do understand if you want to ring round other petsitters to find someone else'.

This usually works but if they are very determined and come back with, for instance, 'My neighbour only has to pay £7 to have her cat fed, why are you charging £10?' Don't answer; 'That's because her cat sitter isn't insured/registered/for tax/police checked or that she isn't recommended by her local vet and she only spends ten minutes in the house.' Just grit your teeth and smile and repeat again: 'As I said, these are my rates …'

I used to try to explain to clients about my petrol costs, wear and tear on my car, how much insurance I had to pay, how well trained I was, the pet first aid courses, behavioural courses, etc. But this only keeps the argument open. It is your business. They don't have to hire you and you certainly don't have to take them on as clients. You can be as picky as you like.

TIP Tell people you have a waiting list. This makes you look in demand even if you're not, and you don't have to turn someone down flat. Before suggesting they go on your list, though, try your hardest to find them another petsitter who you feel comfortable recommending. The fact that you have tried to help them, with no financial gain to yourself, is a great recommendation for your business.

Your Vehicle

If you are only going to be doing pet visits, then you don't have to worry about the size of your car. You will want a vehicle, however, which runs as economically as possible because even if you only intend to cover a small area, you will be stopping and starting a lot, which uses more fuel than longer runs.

If you are using your vehicle for business, you must insure it appropriately. Ring your insurance company and let them know what kind of business you are setting up and ask for their best rates. Should you have a bump, then you know you are covered but if you haven't declared that you are a petsitter who uses the car to go back and forth to clients' homes, the company may not pay up.

How secure is your car? If you have to leave a dog in a car while you go into an another owner's home to fetch their pet, then you want to know that no one can steal the dog left behind.

Air conditioning isn't a luxury when you're transporting pets, it's an essential. Leaving windows open may cool the car down slightly when you are on the road but once a vehicle is stationary, the inside of a car can become an oven, even if it's overcast or there's a breeze. Dogs quickly develop heat stroke in such conditions and can die in as little as 20 minutes.

You can get air conditioning fitted to any car so if you don't have any, consider increasing your start-up budget to allow for a new car with air conditioning or have your old car adapted.

Determining your policy

Before you set up, think about how you'd like to work. Here are a few points to consider.

☐ What would be the earliest you'd agree to visit a pet and the latest? If you're happy to work later than, say, 6 p.m. or at the weekends, how much will you charge for this?

☐ Will you have a flat rate for clients who've booked you for a couple of weeks or will you charge extra for the weekends included in their booking?

☐ What about pets on medication or with long-term health conditions such as diabetes? Do you have the knowledge to offer care for them too?

☐ How many pets would you include in a pet visit before you charged more?

☐ How much cancellation notice will you require and will you charge a cancellation fee?

☐ Are there any dog breeds you wouldn't feel confident walking?

☐ If you're pet visiting, will you allow shared access to the home? For example, cleaners and workmen?

☐ Will you be the sole carer of a pet in your care or will you allow the clients' friends or family to feed or exercise the pet too?

I found that I didn't have much of a policy until I started and then, as challenges came up, I adjusted my policy and the terms and conditions of my service, accordingly.

Naming your business

Naming your petsitting business is exciting. Somehow it makes it all seem real and emphasizes the fact that you are your own boss. It's your business and you can call it what you like – almost. You may have had a name in your head for some time. I know I did, but before you rush into printing out business cards, make sure that the name, you want isn't already taken. I was very upset to find my chosen name, Paws for Thought, had already been taken. I thought it was so original that no one else would have thought of it but I was wrong. There were loads of pet-related businesses with the same name.

Sometimes people type their preferred business name into a domain search and if it doesn't come up as taken, they feel they can use it. Some business name owners don't actually buy a domain name but nevertheless they have registered the business in that name and possibly trademarked it too.

The same can be said of your logo – if you want one. Design one yourself by all means but follow the above advice to make sure that your lovely picture of a pair of caring hands cradling a pet isn't taken (and that one is.) You can't copy and paste a picture or photograph from another website either, even if it's on Google Images – unless it specifically states that the graphic is free. Most clipart is copyright-free too, but always check before using.

If you're artistic this is the perfect opportunity for you to put your talent to good use and save the money that you might have spent on a graphic designer.

Clients will be more likely to remember your petsitting service if the name is easy to remember. Karen's Cat Care Service may not be very exciting but it is personal and easy to remember – if it's available, that is.

This should be a really fun part of starting up your business so with a bit of research and patience, you should find the perfect name and I would advise you to protect it as soon as you are able.

To trademark your business name, go to the Intellectual Property Office, www.ipo.gov. uk/tm.htm.

Long before the internet, a playgroup I sent my son to changed its name to Minnie Mouse's Playschool. In those days there was not much chance of Disney knowing or caring about a small playgroup in North Cornwall using the name of one of its characters. Or so they thought, until one day they received a letter from the Disney Corporation explaining, very nicely, why they couldn't use a Disney name. This shows how far a trademark owner will go to protect their business name.

If you need a boarding or dog walking licence and haven't yet applied, then do it immediately, so that you have time to put into place any changes that the council inspector may require for you to start trading.

It could only happen to a petsitter ...

Joanne, a petsitter colleague, was walking a large dalmatian every day. The dog lived with his single male owner in a mobile home. This particular morning she struggled with the front door key, causing Brutus, the dog, to become more and more agitated. Finally she got in but couldn't calm Brutus down enough to put his collar on. They ended up in the bedroom, where to Joanne's dismay, there was the owner – in bed. Now beside himself with joy at having his two favourite people, his owner and his dog walker, in the same room, Brutus started leaping up and down on the bed. On the third leap, he bounced his stark-naked owner right out of bed onto the floor in front of Joanne.

6
ADVERTISING

In this chapter:

- ☐ Advertising by word of mouth

- ☐ Choosing advertising tools

- ☐ Going to the vets

- ☐ Having a website

- ☐ Using the press

- ☐ Advertising on radio and TV

- ☐ Writing newspapers, blogs and ezines.

You may have the best business in the world but if nobody knows about you, you're going to take much longer to be successful.

Advertising by word of mouth

The good news is that it doesn't have to cost the earth. In fact the oldest form of advertising is still the best: word of mouth. But if you've just started up how can anyone recommend you? So you need to get your petsitting service noticed and the best way is to use a combination of methods.

Not only is advertising vital to your business, it can be a really fun part of it too. If you think creatively you can put together an advertising campaign almost single-handedly.

You may already have looked at the databases of advertising and marketing companies and probably the Yellow Pages too. My advice is: don't commit yourself to anything yet, no matter how attractive their deals sound. Give yourself a bit of time to see what you can do for yourself first. To do this, put yourself in the position of a prospective client. Where would you look first to find professional care for your pets?

For most people this is usually how they search for a petsitter:

- ☐ ask other pet owners

- ☐ call or visit their local vets

□ search the internet

□ read the notice boards in the pet shop

□ read the Yellow Pages or more localized directories.

The order of how people search for information might vary – younger pet owners might look on the web and possibly look in the telephone directory as a last resort. More and more people, though, whatever their age, turn to the internet to look for help.

Before we go through the above list, let's get you into the best frame of mind, with the best advertising tools to sell your business, which, at this stage, means selling you.

You don't have to suddenly turn into Alan Sugar. You can let your business cards, leaflets or brochures do most of the work but you do have to dress the part – and smile.

Choosing advertising tools

Here's a list of the advertising tools which I found most useful when I was trying to drum up business in my local area:

□ business cards

□ three-fold leaflets or brochures

□ postcards

□ baseball hat embroidered with my logo

□ removable magnetic signs for my car

□ small packets of gluten-free pet treats for handing out to pet owners.

BUSINESS CARDS

Business cards, postcards, three-fold leaflets and brochures can be made very easily on your computer. If you go to www.microsoft.com and look up 'templates', you'll find a very wide range of business card templates which are free to download.

I also use VistaPrint, www.vistaprint.com . From here, you can often order your first set of business cards or postcards free of charge, apart from the postage. This, in my opinion, is really worth doing because although my postage came to over £5 (they are produced overseas), the quality of the 50 postcards, delivered in less than ten days, was excellent. Using their interactive website, you simply register and then either use one of their templates or design one using their artwork. I chose a cat and a dog and customized it with my logo and contact details.

Whatever design you use, if you have a superb picture of a pet covering 80% of the card, you can't go wrong. Remember the cards you've seen? Most of them make the same mistake

– the text is too small and overlong. You are only looking to attract someone to your card – not explain everything about your business on it. Having a gorgeous dog and a couple of lines of 32–36pt font, means your ad can be read from a few feet away as people walk past. You'd stop and read a card, if it featured a sweet cat or happy dog, wouldn't you?

The only information you really need on a business card or postcard is: your business name, your telephone number and an email or web address.

BASEBALL CAPS

You could have anything or everything you wear emblazoned with your logo, but I chose a baseball cap as it's relatively inexpensive to buy and there are wealth of companies out there who will print your logo for you. If you do have a company near you, that is ideal as later on you may want sweatshirts and fleeces with your company name and it's good to be able to go and try them out first. If not, the internet is full of companies offering this service. Find one you like, check there's no minimum order as many keep their prices so low by supplying big organizations. Then order your caps or whatever you like.

REMOVABLE MAGNETIC VEHICLE SIGNS

The great thing about removable magnetic signs is that you can chose when and when not to advertise the fact that you are a petsitter. They are also much cheaper than having a logo painted on your vehicle and you can use them for more than one car or van. My most important reason for using them, though, is that because you can remove them, you can visit clients' homes without drawing attention to the fact that the property may be unoccupied. You can create a good, professional impression by wearing or driving your business name but when you are actually working, leave your cap, fleeces and signs hidden in your vehicle.

SMALL GLUTEN FREE-PET TREATS

These may be expensive for what they are and you could easily make them at home but you would have to ensure that they were eaten within a few days. Food hygiene laws apply to animals as well as humans so save the hand-made ones, and your time, for Christmas and birthdays.

By buying gluten-free treats, you are almost eliminating any reactions a pet might have to wheat – the common allergy.

When you start petsitting, you will find it snowballs and you meet more and more pet owners. By having some tasty treats on you, which you (of course) always ask permission from the owner before offering them to the pet, you will make friends with both the owner and the pet. If the dog likes them, not only will he associate you with them (great if you are asked to walk him), but you can offer the owners a few, with your business card, to take home.

Going to the vets

The veterinary surgery is still often your first port of call. You can't do anything about the fact that you are new and that possibly the vet or the receptionist has a petsitter they usually refer people to. You can, however, give yourself a chance to become better known to the surgery staff by going and introducing yourself to them. Now is not the time to be shy; but don't worry, I have always found vet's receptionists and vet nurses to be friendly and chatty, if they have time. With that in mind, pick a time when the surgery is likely to be quieter. Don't go between 8 a.m. and 12 p.m. as they are usually packed with customers and you'll be lucky to talk for more than a minute without the surgery phone interrupting you. Most vets perform operations after 2 p.m. so the ideal time would be 1 p.m. – 2 p.m. Although most of the staff will be having a well-earned break, there will always be someone covering the reception area.

I wouldn't ask to speak to the vet. She (I use 'she' and not 'him' because my vet and her staff are all female) is probably trying to have a few bites of a sandwich and you won't endear yourself to her. Instead take some business cards and a couple of packets of dog or cat treats. Most receptionists and nurses have pets of their own. Some might call this bribery. I like to think of it as more an apple for the teacher. Smile! Remember you need to allow yourself just a few minutes to impress her so ask if you might leave a few cards and brochures with them. At this stage I wouldn't ask if you can have a space on the counter for a brochure or leaflet holder, especially if you see that another petsitter has done this. Your mission at this stage is more relationship building than hard sell.

If you are lucky, there may already be a notice board where you can put your eye-catching card. You may find that your name is simply added to a list or your beautiful brochure is slipped into a waiting-room file for customers to browse through. Don't let this get you down because once you've proven yourself as a reliable, caring petsitter, you will be one of the chosen few and your veterinary surgery feels happy passing your details on to their clients.

Having a website

In the 21st century, most clients will expect you to have a website, even if it's just one page. By having a website you can:

☐ let pet owners see at a glance if you cover their area and provide the services they need

☐ display as much or as little information about your business as you like but you should show the services you offer and the area you cover plus, of course, a variety of ways that potential clients can contact you

☐ put your prices on your site so owners know before they contact you how much you charge (this is useful if you find discussing prices difficult)

☐ submit your site to search engines

☐ accept bookings and payments online – this saves you paperwork and by having a calendar of booked days, clients can see at a glance when you have free slots.

You only need a little knowledge – just how to add content to your website – and you're up and running. This really couldn't be easier as you can now buy a domain name for under a fiver and a ready-made website for under £100.

If you surf the net – and now's the time to do it as you'll be too busy later – you'll find many sites where you can add your business details, often for no fee, such as gum tree, www.gumtree.co.uk. You can also link to other pet-related websites and ask that they link back to you.

A word of caution: you don't want to put anything on a website that you wouldn't feel happy to let the whole world know. Check with pet owners if you want to put their pets' photos on your site. Don't put your home address; your business email address is enough and if you are lucky enough to look like a teenager, please don't put your own photograph up as you may get asked if you offer more than dog walking.

Keep it simple. People's attention span when reading websites is very short. They often won't scroll down, so have just a few lines of text in a large, clear font. As with the postcards, having a picture of a pet catches the eye and can make your website stand out. You can get free pictures from Clipart, www.clipart or, for a few pounds, buy stunning images from somewhere such as Fotolia, www.fotolia.co.uk.

Your website should portray you as a pet lover who is experienced and knowledgeable about the type of animals you are offering to care for.

Using the press

When I started petsitting, my brother, who works for an advertising agency in America, scared me to death when he suggested I send out a 'media pack' to all and sundry. When I looked baffled, he said, 'you know, press releases, etc.' I thought press releases were something politicians sent out to newspaper editors denying their involvement in arms deals or models' arms!

A press release is really nothing more than a cunningly concealed advertisement for your business. The trick is to make it something that a reader, radio listener or television viewer, would find interesting.

To write a press release, there are a few points to remember.

☐ Include all your contact details so the paper can reach you if they need more information or want to use their own photographer to take photos of you.

☐ Type at the top of your text, 'For immediate release'.

☐ Keep it very brief, usually no longer than half an A4 page.

□ Include a photo – pictures really are worth a thousand words.

□ Make it newsworthy, informative and above all, it should not read as an advertisement for you – although it is!

Here is a fictional press release you can use as a template or if you are unsure what to write. You can probably do much better than this but feel free to copy it as it is or customize it to suit you.

Date:

Business Name:

Email;

Website:

Contact:

FOR IMMEDIATE RELEASE

'While Their Owners are Away the Cats can play!'

The cat owners of Guildford no longer have to risk scratched arms and flying fur, getting their cats in cat boxes ready for a stay in a cattery. Cool for Cats, a service dedicated to looking after home-alone cats, has just opened. Business owner, Chloe Peters, says:

'I got the idea after I'd had enough of leaving guilty cat faces behind me. I realized that if I felt like this, then so must other cat owners so I set up Cool for Cats. The response has been amazing and I get a lot of satisfaction from knowing that I am giving owners peace of mind. My clients' cats are happy staying in familiar surrounds with a daily or twice daily visit to be fed, litter clean and above all, receive lots of TLC.' Chloe has just built her own website where you can find and even book your cat's holidays, www.chloescool4cats.co.uk

---

Before you send your press release out into the world, spend some time finding out the names of the right people on the newspaper/radio or TV station to send it to. Ring the paper and ask the advice of the receptionist. They may suggest the news desk or the desk of which ever journalist covers the pet or local community section.

Remember that a good photograph of you with a pet or two and perhaps a happy owner really will triple your press release's chances. If you have seen other petsitters featured in the same newspaper then don't imagine readers won't be interested in yours. You just have to find a different slant. Maybe you're an expert on parrots? Or perhaps you have an interest in dog behaviour or senior pets? Do you offer microchipping or dog grooming as an extra service? You can always find something original about your business.

Advertising on radio and TV

If you send your press releases to a few local radio stations, they may well contact you to see if you'd like to chat to one their presenters, on air, about your exciting new business. I actually accosted a presenter from my local radio station while they were covering another story, outside Sainsburys. I gave her one of my business cards which had an enormous rabbit on it and started waffling nervously about petsitting. The sweet presenter thanked me and said she might be in touch. Of course I dismissed this and was shocked but pleased to receive a call from her a few days later. I then nearly ruined it by trying to talk her out of interviewing me because I was terrified. She explained that it would just be a ten-minute chat. I told her I couldn't possibly talk for ten minutes on air. She explained we would go through all the questions beforehand and if I stalled, she would cover for me.

In the end we did it and although I sounded like Minnie Mouse, I must admit I was very pleased I'd done it. The next week, I'd taken on five more bookings, one of which was a lovely dog of nearly 16 and I cared for him until he died at the grand old age of 19.

Writing newsletters, blogs and ezines

Writing a regular newsletter or ezine for your clients is a great way of advertising. Don't commit yourself to a monthly or even bimonthly one unless you have the time – a quarterly newsletter can not only inform your clients of changes of policy within your business and price increases but can be used to help them care for their pets by including pet-related articles. These can be as short or long as you like. You might include warnings about adders in the summer, dog walks you know of which your dog-owning clients might not have discovered yet, your achievements such as becoming pet first aid qualified or gaining a diploma in cat behaviour.

Try writing a few short articles for the local community paper or school newsletters. See if you can leave a few copies with your vet, your doctors – anywhere people congregate, along with some business cards.

By making yourself known to other pet professionals and business people, you will be networking – one of the greatest assets to any business.

Don't use negative advertising. By this I mean running down your competition. This is unprofessional and may well backfire on you. I've seen websites featuring graphics of a dog behind bars. This type of advertising simply brings down our profession and reflects badly on petsitters. By the same token, if anyone asks for your opinion on another petsitter, then if she's good, say so and if not, say nothing.

Blogs and ezines are simply newsletters which you produce on your PC and then send out via email to those of your customers who have agreed to receive them. No matter how good they are, you wouldn't want to spam anyone. I usually put them in the body of an email rather than as an attachment as, even if you have an all-singing, all-dancing anti-virus programme, it is still safer to deliver them this way. Besides which, downloading attachments takes longer and people don't always have the time to do this.

It could only happen to a petsitter...

Michelle, a petsitter in the next village to me, had a lovely assignment popping in to care for a Russian blue cat twice a day for three weeks while the cat's owners were on holiday in Greece. The cat, Cleo, was a house cat and the apple of her owner's eye. She had a bed in every room of the very large house and hundreds of toys too.

This particular day, Michelle tripped as she left the house after spending an hour playing with Cleo. Cleo took the opportunity to dash out of the front door and ran behind the house and up a large oak tree.

Michelle tried everything she could to get Cleo down but she wouldn't budge. It was summer but by 9 p.m., it was starting to get dark and Michelle was really worried by now that Cleo would fall if she tried to jump down. After consulting with the owners, Michelle rang the fire service who came out and rescued Cleo. And the happy ending? Michelle found herself being invited out to dinner by the tallest, best-looking fireman in Berkshire.

7
PETSITTING BUSINESS FORMS

In this chapter:

- ☐ Pet information questionnaire
- ☐ Service contract
- ☐ Vet authority
- ☐ Key release/locksmith permission
- ☐ Cat flap disclaimer
- ☐ Permission to enter house
- ☐ House alarms
- ☐ Neighbour notification card
- ☐ Booking confirmation
- ☐ Repeat booking form
- ☐ Invoices
- ☐ Service evaluation form
- ☐ Daily pet visit log
- ☐ Medical forms
- ☐ Checklist for clients
- ☐ Sample forms.

Your forms are a vital part of your business. Don't put off buying or designing your own forms because not only can they provide vital information about your clients and their pets, they can help protect you from legal action.

This list of petsitting business forms may seem long but you can integrate many of them into one form. Below each heading is a brief explanation of the reason for the form.

Pet information questionnaire

I use information forms to record as much as possible about the pets. This is (usually) filled in by the customer and checked by me.

Everything you'll need to know about the pet you're going to care for should be detailed here. You'll want to know its breed, gender and age. Has the pet been neutered? How often should it be exercised, fed and cleaned? Where will you find its food and bedding supplies? Does it like to be handled? Is it frightened or worried by anything? Don't be afraid to ask as many questions as you feel you need to. 'Less is more' doesn't work here.

Service contract

Contracts are necessary to form a legal agreement between you and the customer. This agreement states your obligations in providing a petsitting service and what the customer's obligations are in providing correct information about their pets, home and other relevant details. And importantly, it states payment of your fees according to your payment policy.

You can pay a lawyer to draw up contracts for you. This may cost at least a few hundred pounds. If a lawyer hasn't drawn these up from scratch, then you can ask them to look over a contract which you've put together or bought ready-made.

I think that the most important thing to remember about a contract is that both parties must sign it for it to become legally binding.

Vet authority

Have signed permission from your client to take his pet to a vet (stipulate that you will use any vet if it's an emergency and his own vet isn't available). The form should also state that the client, not you, will be liable for payment of all fees and that these fees are to be settled by the client.

Key release/locksmith permission

If you keep your clients' keys in your possession, make sure you have the clients' written permission.

Cat flap disclaimer

Clients' cats are far safer if they are kept indoors while you care for them but if they insist that they be allowed access to a cat flap (never anything else, i.e. open windows), then having a disclaimer should cover you.

Permission to enter house

I use this as a simple card, like a 'doctor on call' sign. Placed in view by the windscreen, it reassures neighbours especially if used in conjunction with the neighbour notification cards. If you are ever challenged by the police during a petsitting visit, it's handy to have this as well as some ID.

House alarms

Many homes have house alarms, all with different modes of operation. Information about the location of the alarm, how to turn it on and off, contact details of the alarm company and a reminder for the clients to notify this company that they have hired you, should all be recorded along with the most important thing – the code.

Neighbour notification card

This could be a postcard-sized form which the client can use to inform his neighbours that you will be caring for your client's pets in their absence. Your contact details should be stated and the dates you'll be visiting the property.

Booking confirmation

Once you've arranged a booking, send an email or letter confirming the booking and stating the exact dates you're booking for. This should include the start day and the last day of service. Putting 'from 27 January to 3 February', for example, leaves too much room for error. Are you expected to start on the 27th or the 28th of January and is the 2nd of February your last day or the 3rd?

Repeat booking form

For regular customers, you don't want them to have to fill in a whole new contract every time they use you so using a repeat booking form to act as a contract in itself, works for me. You state in the booking form that you are providing care under the terms of the original contract and that you must be informed of any changes.

You should find you built a good base of clients who re-book you frequently. Neither you nor they will want to fill out a new contract and pet information form every time they re-book so use re-booking forms instead. On your original contract, word it so that the original contract is valid for all repeat bookings provided there have been no changes in circumstances – the pet might now be on medication or there might even be a new pet in the family.

I was amazed by how many people who casually mention when re-booking me, that they had an extra dog, cat or other pet. If any of your clients do acquire an extra pet, then you always have to visit them and see the pet for yourself – really a repeat of your first consultation with them.

I have turned up at homes to find a fish tank brimming over with tropical fish which the owner had forgotten to tell me she'd bought. Another family had rescued a cat and didn't mention it to me. The poor cat and I got quite a shock. Once I went to walk a couple of dogs after I'd taken a holiday and found only one dog – the owners hadn't told me that the other had died, which I found very upsetting, as you do grow to love these pets almost as much as your own.

So always send or email a re-booking form and once you receive it, send out your confirmation email or letter.

Invoices

When you send repeat booking forms to regular customers, you can integrate invoices into them to save time and paper. www.microsoft.com has some excellent invoice templates on their website. You can easily customize these to suit your business.

Service evaluation form

Scary? A bit to begin with! However, do try leaving these in your clients' homes on your last petsitting visit. You may be pleasantly surprised with the compliments you receive and any negative feedback shouldn't be taken personally. It's a good way to learn how you can improve your service.

You will always get one client, though, who takes great delight in listing a whole host of ridiculous things they feel you should have done. If they are being petty and you know you've done a great job, then you can take great delight in turning them down next time they try to book you. If you feel they've got a point – or a few points, then act on them and you'll be more respected for it.

Daily pet visit log

Dog owners, especially, love to come back and read accounts of their dog's adventures in their absence so I often leave additional notes as well as my daily dog log. I put check boxes in for the 'Vitals: Poos and wees!'.

By keeping a record of every pet visit or dog walk, you, and your client, always have something to refer back to if needed. This could be vital in tracking exactly when a dog, for example, started limping or when a cat refused her food. It is also a great way of building a rapport with the pet's owner. It doesn't have to be a detailed account every day – just a note saying you've visited will do – but most owners really appreciate a more personal account of how their pet has spent its time with you.

My pet logs for pet visiting are made up horizontally on A4 size paper. Using Microsoft Word or Excel, I add columns for the date, the day, the time in and time out, a longer box for 'description of visit', another column for food and a final column for medication administered. If the pet is on medication though, I also have two more detailed forms: pet medical history and permission to administer medication.

Medical forms

Either integrate these with the pet information form or use as separate forms, but whatever you do, have them. You need to know past illnesses, injuries, treatments, symptoms to watch out for, medications prescribed, contraindications (bad reactions to medication), and present medication. You'll also need to know dosages and time, if applicable, to administer it.

Try to always have not only the owner's instructions but the vet's as well in case the owners accidentally write the wrong data down for you. Ask to be left the printout the owners would have received at the surgery. They may not still have this but if you always ask that the medicine's packaging be left out for you, this should have the exact instructions for use printed on the boxes. Take your time reading the instructions – you'll want to be 100% certain that you understand them.

If you have more than one pet to look after, then ask the owners to put collars and name tags on them. Of course you can't do this with birds or fish but it is the best way for cats and dogs. Also, put a copy of the photograph you or the owner took of the pet before you started caring for them (as mentioned in Chapter 8), and write on a sticky label, for example: 'Molly has one in the morning and two at night.' Stick this on the photo of Molly and then you can refer to it.

I once looked after three identical-looking cats. They were all elderly and all on different medication. To distinguish between them I noted down that TJ had a white flash on his chest and that Bruno had a tuft of hair missing by his ear. This worked fine until the third cat, Frankie, got into a fight and then also had a tuft of fur missing by his ear. The next time I visited them, I insisted that the owners put collars and name tags on them.

Checklist for clients

Some petsitters leave checklists for clients and I think this is an excellent idea. The client checks off whether they have left enough food and necessary medication for their pets, that the temperature of the house is adequate for their pets and you – see Chapter 4, 'Legal, health and safety' – and any other factors, you think helpful.

The most important check of all is for them to count their pets before they go. I once visited a house with four cats and found one of them had been shut in the bathroom for six hours since the owners had left. Suffice to say, he hadn't used the loo but he had used what seemed like every other part of the room.

Sample forms

The six forms below include a basic pet visiting contract, pet information form, permission to administer medicine, pet daily log, cat flap disclaimer and a sample dog-walking terms and conditions. Feel free to copy them in their entirety, changing or adding anything pertinent to your business. These forms have served me well and have been checked over by a lawyer but I accept no liability for them and you must always get a lawyer to check over your own forms.

| Logo | PET VISITING CONTRACT | Your address |

Owners Name ....

Pets Name ....

Address ....

.... Post Code ....

Home Telephone .... Mob ....

Email ....

EMERGENCY CONTACT DETAILS

Should we not be able to contact you, please list a person who can make a decision concerning your pet and your property, in your absence. This could mean a decision regarding medical treatment such as emergency or euthanasia. Please ensure your named person knows that you have nominated them

Name.. Relationship...

Tel.. Mob ....

Property Security

All visitors to your property, must sign a Visitors Log when entering. I.e. cleaners & painters

I understand that no liability can be attached to..................... If a third party share access to my property or pets

KEYS

I have released a set of house keys (1 back door and 1 front door)

I wish...................... ....to retain a set of my keys Y/N

Client Sign...

Petsitter sign...

We will only give your keys back to the above client signed key holder, at the end of our contract stated below.

Veterinary Authorisation Details

Vets Name.......................................

Address...

Tel No.......................................

During my absence, I have given permission for................................to act as a guardian for my pets named above, I AUTHORISE THE ABOVE VETS TO TREAT MY PETS IN CASE OF ANY ILLNESS.
I will be responsible for any vets charges that may be incurred.
Please take any action suitable in order to keep my pets in good health.
I give the pet carer permission to transport the above pets to the named vets.
In agree that in the event of surgery or euthanasia the petsitter will accept the advice of the vet and the above emergency contact will be contacted.

Signed...

PET VISITING CONTRACT/2

I AUTHORISE .... ANY ACTION THAT THEY CONSIDER SUITABLE IN ORDER TO PROTECT AND KEEP MY PET IN GOOD HEALTH

I CONFIRM THAT I WILL BE RESPONSIBLE FOR ANY COSTS WHICH MIGHT BE INCURRED, EITHER VETERINARY OR OTHER, AS A RESULT OF ANY SICKNESS, ACCIDENT OR DAMAGE CAUSED TO OR BY THE ABOVE NAMED PET(S), EXCEPTING THIRD PARTY LIABILITY, AND THAT I WILL PAY ANY SUCH COSTS OR EXPENSES ON DEMAND. I ALSO UNDERSTAND THAT NO LIABILITY WILL ATTACH TO THE PETSITTER.

I wish my pet to be walked / cared for on the following days:

Am Mon [ ]   Tues [ ]   Wed [ ]   Thurs [ ]   Fri [ ]

Pm Mon [ ]   Tues [ ]   Wed [ ]   Thurs [ ]   Fri [ ]

Dog walking times 11am – 2.30pm

Cat calls 9.00am – 11.00am & 4.00pm – 6.00pm

FULL PAYMENT REQUIRED BEFORE START OF SERVICE

I agree to pay the fee of £............................   (Please see price list)

First day of services:...................................   **Last day of service**.............................

Approx departure time ....   **Approx arrival time**.........................

PLEASE CONTACT US ON YOUR RETURN FROM YOUR HOLIDAY OR WE WILL CHARGE FOR ADDITIONAL VISITS

Start of holiday if applicable...........................   **End of holiday if applicable**.............................

Clients Name......................................   **Clients Signature**.....................................

Petsitter Signature ....   **Date**.................................

Logo	PET INFORMATION FORM	Your address

Owners Name ....

Pets Name ....
Age .... Gender ....
Chipped? **Y/N** Neutered? **Y/N**

Please Attach a Photo of your Pet here:

Name & Address of your Veterinary Surgery...

....

....

.... Post Code...................Tel............................

Does your pet live outside or inside?...........................

If inside does he have outside access such as a day run? **Y/N**.

Do they wear ID tags? **Y/N**

Favourite hiding places?...

Location of pet's food ....

Amount given at each visit?...........................

Does the pet have treats and/or fresh fruit & veg and if so how much daily?

....

Do we need to give your pet any medication or treatment? **Y/N**

Please fill out a 'Permission to Administer Medication' Form if your pets need daily medication

Where will we find bedding/straw/hay...

....

PET INFORMATION FORM/2

Bin bags........................... Dustpan/brush/vacuum cleaner......................................

What words or cue do you use to call your pet?...

Does your pet like to be handled? **Y/N**. Playing games? **Y/N**

If yes please specify ....

Is your pet worried by or dislikes anything that we should be aware of?

....

List any other information here such as plants you would like watered. Please ensure water damage is not possible – i.e. move plants off carpets/wood floors.

Bin Collection day? .... Where is your bin collected from? ....

Where shall we put your post or deliveries? ....

Security Information

Have you informed your neighbours that we will be caring for your pet? **Y/N**

Please list any further information to help us care for your pets, overleaf.

Thank you.

CAT OUTSIDE ACCESS DISCLAIMER (CAT FLAPS)

Although it is always safer to keep cats indoors during their owners' absence, we appreciate that this is not for everyone and as you are aware of the risks, we will care for your cat/s while he has access to a cat flap.

Disclaimer

'Your Company' cannot be held responsible for any loss of pets who have access to an open cat flap.

In the event of your pet going missing, we will continue to provide care visits for your cats until your return.

We will notify your Emergency Contact, your vet and the relevant authorities that your pet is missing from home.

This Authority is valid for this and any future booking I make with 'Your Company'

I, (Client Name)   agree that 'Your Company' cannot be held liable for the loss of my cat/s while they have access to an unlocked cat flap.

Client Signature...Date.........................

PERMISSION TO ADMINISTER MEDICINE

Pet's Name...Attach photo of pet to form.

Name of Medicine..

How administered?..

Dose..................... How many times per day? ....

Times to administer medicine: (This should be within a two hour window because of our other petsitting duties and the possibility of delay)

Am......................... Pm...........................

Other times...

Please leave the complete container and instructions as printed on them by the VET to eliminate error.

Where will we find the medicine?...

Vet's Contact Details..

I authorise (your company) to administer the stated medication to the above named pet for the duration of my absence and there after whenever (your company) cares for this pet, until I revoke or change this permission.

Client Name...

Client Signature...Date..................

DAILY PET LOG

Pets Names: Misty and Bramble

First Day Service .... to Last Day of Service ....

Day	Time	Time Out	Food and/or Medication	Description of Visit

SAMPLE DOG WALKING TERMS AND CONDITIONS

Acceptance of our services is deemed acceptance of our Terms and Conditions and an agreement to pay our fees on time.

We reserve the right to stop walking a dog if he shows aggression to people or other dogs.

We reserve the right to either impose supplementary charges and/or terminate this agreement if, the assignment changes from the description given by the client and needs more time or responsibility or if there is a change in the nature of the assignment which could not have been reasonably foreseen by either party.

We will not be liable for any damage or injury caused by your dog excepting that of proven Third Party. There is always an hour window of time allowed to pick up and drop off your dog—i.e., a 10am pick up can mean a 9am or 11am pick up.

We cannot be held liable for any theft or damage to your property or injury/illness to your pet unless we can be shown to be negligent.

We reserve the right to deny or terminate service because of safety or financial concerns.

Extreme weather conditions may mean a curtailment or cancellation of our services at short notice. (We will keep your pet company if we can get there.)

We will try to give 24hrs notice if we cannot walk your dog. If not, we will refund the fee for that walk.

If 24 hrs notice is not given by the client of cancellation, we reserve the right to charge for that walk.

We do not walk dogs during thunderstorms or extreme heat but will let your dog out to relieve himself and keep him company indoors.

We cannot walk ill dogs or dogs known to have an infection even on a one to one basis because of the risk of cross infection.

We will not feed deep chested dogs in the hour presiding or after a walk because of the risk to your dog of gastric torsion.

Kennel Cough

Although every care is taken to prevent contact with dogs with kennel cough, the incubation period means that it is always possible your dog may pick this up and we cannot be held liable for your dog contacting kennel cough. We strongly advise you discuss kennel cough vaccination with your vet.

We will not walk dogs who wear choke chains or electric collars nor can we administer negative punishment (smacking or jerking collars or any method which may cause the dog pain or distress).

Holidays

We aim to give you six weeks notice at least, of our holidays.

Weekly bookings are greatly discounted and need to be paid one week in advance. You are paying for the whole week at a greatly discounted rate so we cannot refund for part week should you not need us. If you do not need us for the following week, we cannot guarantee to have space for your pet without a retainer (50% of your normal weekly fee—per week).

We are always happy to visit you to see if our services may be right for you – although we cannot confirm dog walking or puppy visits without a firm booking date with one weeks deposit.

Should we not be able to fulfill a walk or visit ourselves or with one of our outside contractors, we will refund for that/those walks or visits.

8
INITIAL CLIENT CONSULTATION

In this chapter:

- ☐ Preparing for the consultation
- ☐ Meeting the clients
- ☐ Carrying out the home check
- ☐ Checking house security
- ☐ Going through the paperwork
- ☐ Checking medical history, feeding and care routine
- ☐ Answering client's questions
- ☐ Before you leave
- ☐ Confirming the booking.

Preparing for consultation

First of all, don't worry. It's normal to feel some trepidation before your first client consultation. After all, it's not every day you're interviewed by a couple and their pet. Remember that they will probably be anxious too. They may not have left their pet before and it's part of your job to reassure them.

In the example below, I've described a client consultation with a couple looking for care for their cats and their rabbit while they are on holiday. This example covers most small animals. (The consultation with a dog owner is different; this is covered in Chapter 11, 'Dog walking'.)

Before you leave your house, do a quick check to make sure you have everything you need in your bag:

- ☐ pet information sheets and contracts – and some spares
- ☐ a new client folder
- ☐ your own checklist and notebook

☐ your portfolio, which should include a copy of your insurance policy, police clearance report, references, press cuttings and perhaps photographs of other pets you care for

☐ some pet treats – but check that the animals are allowed treats before offering them

☐ your mobile phone.

Meeting the clients

When you arrive at the home of your potential clients, they may offer you coffee or a tea. It's better to refuse politely, especially if you are nervous, in case you spill it, as I did on my very first interview – a good reason to take spare paperwork with you.

The animals should be there when you arrive. Don't make too much fuss of them or encourage them to come to you if they are shy. Instead, kneel down and offer them your hand to smell. The owners will want to see how their pets react to you, but don't insist they catch them to bring them to you. Suggest instead that the animals get used to hearing your voice first. Say that later, if possible, you would like to do a quick 'head to tail' assessment – but only if the cats are happy about this.

You do need to see the pets at some point, of course, as you will want to satisfy yourself that they show no obvious signs of ill health. Also, if the owner has not already provided one, you might like to take a photograph for your records or in case the pet goes missing.

Carrying out the home check

Ask to be shown round the part of the house that the cats will have access to, and note if any rooms are to be off-limits to them. The paperwork already completed will cover how much food the pets should have, when they are fed, cat litter and care routine, but you need to see the following in particular.

☐ Where the food, feeding bowls, cat litter, straw, hay, etc., are kept.

☐ If any of the pets need medicine, you need to know where this, and the measuring spoon or syringe, are kept.

☐ Which cutlery and tea towels you should use for the pets.

☐ Where any cleaning materials are kept and which are safe to use.

☐ Which bin you should use for uneaten food and soiled litter, and where the main dustbin is located.

☐ Which taps you can use for the pets' water. (Some people have a softened household water supply which is unsuitable for drinking.)

☐ Broom, dustpan and vacuum cleaner.

☐ Where the fuse box and stopcock are located in case of a power failure or burst pipe.

☐ The thermostat, so that you can turn the heating up or down if necessary.

☐ If they have requested that you water plants, ask to see them and remind owners to group them together, if possible, on a waterproof surface. (You don't want to be responsible for a ruined rug.)

☐ Whether curtains are to be drawn and/or lights put on to make the home appear occupied.

Use your clipboard to make notes and to fill in blank areas of the pet information form.

Checking house security

As you walk round, be aware of your own safety requirements too. You need to be able to leave quickly in an emergency, so make sure you will have access to a back-door key, which you should test; and if any of the doors are bolted, check you can undo them easily.

If the owners use a house alarm, they should have filled in the details on your form. If not, you can fill it in while they show you where the alarm is situated and how to set and unset it. It's a great idea if they can change the code to one that's easy for you to remember; if this isn't possible, make sure the code is on the information form, and in another safe place as a back-up: your mobile phone, for instance.

You will need to know how to cancel the alarm should it go off by mistake, and how to reset it correctly. If they haven't written it down already, ask the owners for the contact details of the alarm company, in case of emergency, and suggest they pass on your details to the company so that you can identify yourself easily to them.

Many house alarms log enter and exit times.

Remember this when you fill out your Daily Pet Log – if you've said you've been there for an hour and the alarm records say different, you might not get booked again!

THE GARDEN

If the pets have access to the garden, go outside to check for any holes in the fence or anything which could be dangerous.

Check the condition and size of the rabbit hutch. Are you happy that the hutch is big enough for the rabbit? One of the biggest threats to domestic rabbits is the urban fox. Is the rabbit adequately protected? If you find that the hutch is in need of repair or the size is inappropriate, discuss this in a friendly and diplomatic way and work out a solution with the owners. The majority of pet owners look after their pets wonderfully and care deeply about them; that's why they've booked you, after all. So if you come across a pet who is being kept in less comfortable surroundings, it is usually down to ignorance and not through lack of care. A tactful way to raise the subject is this: your trade association insists you work within their guidelines, and you'd like to suggest a couple of changes – a slightly bigger/newer hutch – which will allow you to accept the assignment. Keep smiling – you are there to help them and their pets.

Going through the paperwork

After you've looked around the house, it's time to sit around a table and go through the paperwork. (You can see now why you need to ask your clients to allow at least an hour for your visit.) Don't be afraid to make a charge for this visit, but make it clear it will be refunded if they book you.

PET INFORMATION FORM

When everyone is sitting down, read back the pet information form to the clients. There is often something to clarify, or a point they might have forgotten. Stress that nothing is too small to mention. I had a client whose cat was frightened of people with caps on. He ran away every time he saw me, until my last visit when I wasn't wearing one. When I told the owners that I hadn't been able to cuddle him, they looked at my cap and then at each other. If only they'd told me! They did book me many times after that; I went capless and spent many happy times sitting in the owners' garden with Solomon the Siamese purring on my lap.

VACCINATION CERTIFICATES

You will also want to see the pets' vaccination certificates but if they haven't been able to find them, ask them to get a note from the vet confirming that they are current and up to date. This includes rabbits, who should be vaccinated against myxomatosis and viral haemorrhagic fever.

CAT FLAP DISCLAIMER

For cats which have access to outside, it is particularly important that the owners understand and have signed your outside access liability disclaimer. Of course, it is better for you if you can at least shut the cats inside with a litter box at night, but many owners prefer that the cat has free access at all times. You need to help them weigh up the possible stress to the cat if his liberty is curtailed, against the indisputable fact that some cats do stray when their owners are away, no matter how much they like the petsitter.

Cats are much safer inside if this is possible. If you're making a couple of visits a day, they will have plenty of play time and company. You need to draw up your own policy on this, but if the owners do want the cat to use a cat flap, you cover yourself by ensuring they sign the disclaimer. Explain that should the cat disappear, you will inform the owner and the local vet and anyone else they feel is relevant; and that you will still visit every day to check to see if the cat has returned – so your daily rate will still be payable.

Checking medical history, feeding and care routine

Even if the clients haven't mentioned it, check that the pets aren't taking any medicines or supplements or have any health concerns. For example, if they lick their fur excessively when left alone, you need to know because any coughing could indicate hair balls.

If you are to administer medicine, the clients should fill in the permission to administer medicine form, and you should state in your daily pet log the time and amount of medicine you've given.

Sometimes clients will ask you to do nothing more than pop in every other day to feed their cats: something they may have had a neighbour do for years. This really is not advisable. When a cat doesn't eat for more than 24 hours it can quickly develop idiopathic hepatic lipidosis (fatty liver disease), which can be fatal. Visiting every day, you can check that the cat is eating regularly and if it isn't, take it to the owners' vet. When you explain this to the client, they will see that you have their cats' best interests at heart and are not just out to earn more money. You have a waiting list of clients, don't you? Not yet maybe, but if you are professional, knowledgeable and caring you soon will.

TERMS AND CONDITIONS

Make sure you draw attention to your terms and conditions, which you also included in the information pack. Most people only skim them; point out that they will be agreeing to them when they sign the contract and ask if they have any questions regarding them. You might, perhaps, draw their attention to any you feel particularly pertinent to them; for example, your non-liability for damage caused by their cats, if their sweet little cat has particularly sharp claws and has been busy sharpening them further on the side of the sofa. You might want to suggest they leave a tempting new scratching post, and if they have a sofa or chair which they really don't want to suffer from the attention of cat claws, a few strips of double-sided sticky tape puts the most dedicated scratcher off his stride.

You shouldn't be afraid of suggesting tips to help them. They will expect you to be knowledgeable about your profession after all – but don't get carried away. Pets are as important as children to most pet owners, and they can become defensive if they feel their 'parenting' skills are being challenged.

Answering clients' questions

I used to find that because the concept of petsitting isn't as well known here as in America, owners were often unsure of what questions to ask me. I would sit there aching to show off my portfolio of glowing references from my other clients, my insurance policy and my membership certificate of my trade association, and they'd never ask about any of these. In fact I was amazed and slightly worried by how trusting people were. This was one of the reasons I went on to help form Accredited Petsitters.

So, don't wait to be asked! Show off your credentials with pride and explain how you came by them. Keep it brief, though, and make sure the whole interview has taken no longer than you informed them it would.

PAYMENT

Including your price list in the client information pack ensures your clients know what you charge before the initial interview. They will have decided already that this is a service they can afford, but your interview with them should help them confirm this. Of course they may decide they don't need you after the meeting, or you may have decided they you don't want them. There's nothing you can do about the former, and you would probably know whether you wish to have them as clients from the information you received from them.

But if, for instance, the cat attacked you – very rare but cats have long memories and if they've been hurt by a 6ft blonde before and you're a 6ft blonde – it would be fair to say that the cat would be happier being cared for by someone else or in a cattery.

Before you leave

Provided all parties are happy with the arrangement, ask the clients to sign and date the contract, and add your own signature and date. Then give owners a receipt for any cheques or cash they give you, or tell them you will send a receipt with their booking confirmation.

The last thing to check before you leave your new clients is that you can operate the keys they give you. This may sound odd, but sometimes people get used to the idiosyncrasies of their keys, and they might forget to explain them to you. Make sure you can actually lock and unlock the doors. You should have been given two sets as you requested in your information pack, but if they have forgotten, check with them that you can have another set cut and bill them for it.

During your first consultation with new clients, it is especially important to be knowledgeable, caring and professional. This will make it easier for them to go away and enjoy their holiday, knowing their pets are in safe hands – which, of course, they are.

Confirming the booking

After the consultation, send an email confirming the booking. For example:

Thank you for booking us to care for Sammy and Trixie while you are on holiday.

Our service starts: Date: 27.3.07 Day: Sat Times of visits: 10 am and 2 pm Our last day of service: Date: 2. 4 .07 Day: Sat – 10 am visit only.

9
DAY-TO-DAY PETSITTING

In this chapter:

☐ Typical Schedule

☐ Staying safe

☐ Deciding petsitter attire and accessories.

Typical schedule

Every petsitter's schedule will be different and probably every day will be unlike the day before, but even so, I thought it might be helpful to tell you about a day in the life of a petsitter. This is taken from one of my diaries.

7.30 a.m. – Get myself, husband and children up for breakfast, school and work.

8.30 a.m. – Sit at the breakfast table with a cup of coffee, diary open and the PC humming in the background.

Go through the visits I have to make to today and make sure I have each client's file in front of me.

Read notes again for an initial consultation with a couple with a young weimaraner called Harry. Check my mobile to see if Freddie, a large cat I've been looking after for a fortnight, has got his owners back with him after their holiday in Ireland. There is a text saying that they've arrived home safely and thanking me for caring for Freddie. If they hadn't contacted me to say they were home, I would have gone round this morning to make sure that Freddie was okay…and charged his owners for an extra visit.

9.30 a.m. – Load up my car with two fresh water bottles, one for dogs and one for me. Lay out fresh blankets and a towel in the hatch of my car and check that all the dogs leads are attached to the dog guard.

Drive to my first pet visit with my clients' packs for the morning and keys to the various homes safely attached to my belt.

My first visit is to Purdy, Ralph and Sophie, three short-haired cats, all rescued, who are doted on by their owners but, sadly, don't care much for each other. Because of this I have to feed Purdy outside, Sophie in the kitchen and Ralph in the hall. They are outside cats who have 24-hour access to a cat flap. I find each cat and while they are feeding, I check the post box, open the curtains in the living room and bring in the newspapers.

I check each cat and give them all some individual attention, referring to my notes again to see that Purdy doesn't like being stroked but enjoys games. I play with a toy on a rope with her. Ralph loves having his chest stroked but not his back – no problem – Sophie likes being groomed and fussed over. After 20 minutes administering TLC, I wander out into the garden to check that the fish in the pond are okay and sprinkle a couple of pinches of food in the water, exactly as stated in my notes.

After washing the cats' dishes, I lock the back door, leave by the front door and lock it after me.

10.30 a.m. — My first dog walk of the day. I drive a couple of miles to the next village and collect Charlie, a ten-month-old male black Labrador. Charlie's owners leave him confined with a child gate in a large kitchen with an open crate fitted out with a baby duvet and numerous toys. He's overjoyed to see me as usual and after letting him out for a wee in the garden, he gets into one of the two dog crates in the back of my car before setting off to pick up Pickle, a collie cross who is just a month older than Charlie and a perfect companion for him.

We drive to nearby woods and I spend an hour walking in the sunshine while the dogs chase each other and play hide and seek among the trees.

11.45 a.m — After settling both dogs in at their homes, I pick up two German shepherds from one house and a little Jack Russell from another. The GSDS have a crate each in the back of my car and Max wears a car harness and is strapped into the back seat.

I take them to a large park where we meet another dog walker who I know. She asks me if I can cover some of her work while she's on holiday, which is fine, and we walk together, although Max has to go back on his lead for a while to stop him being over-amorous with Joanne's walked dogs, two collie bitches. I make a mental note to talk to Max's owners again about the benefits of castration!

1 p.m. – Go home, grab a sandwich and pick up my two dogs and walk round the corner to Toby's home. Toby is a 15-year-old mongrel who only needs a 20-minute walk but enjoys the company of other dogs. We spend the rest of the hour visit sitting in his garden while I have a coffee, kindly left ready for me by Toby's owner. My dogs sniff and strut around the garden while I sit and rub Toby's back.

2 p.m. – Visit to a couple of rabbits, Sam and Susan. These large lop bunnies are very affectionate and bright. I put harnesses on them both to walk round the garden. They do have a very large, fox-proof run but it's still good fun for them, and me, to stroll around the flower beds.

I put them back in their run while I clean out their hutches, change their water bottles and then leave them some fresh greens. They have little hay racks which I fill and then put some treats in activity balls for them.

The run is 6ft high and attached to their 'hutch', which is a large Wendy house. I go into the run, sit down and call them to me. It's vital that I check them both daily for signs of flystrike (see Chapter 10, 'Caring for home-alone pets').

3 p.m. – Home in time to greet my children from school and to give my own dogs a long walk.

4 p.m. – Return calls which have been left on both my home answerphone and my mobile.

6 p.m. – Visit two Siamese cats, Oscar and Stan. Stan has diabetes and needs twice – daily insulin injections. His owner left for a business trip this lunch time so I will inject Stan once he has eaten his supper. The house has a burglar alarm. I have the code keyed into my mobile phone, and I turn this off before I see to the cats. I then lock the cat flap to keep them both in for the night and prepare the cats' evening meal. While they're eating, I prepare Stan's insulin injection and administer this while he's eating his last few mouthfuls. I'm so used to doing this, he doesn't even flinch.

After washing their cat bowls and putting fresh water down, I spend 20 minutes cuddling the cats before filling in the pet log, closing the curtains in the living room and leaving a light on to make the place look occupied. After setting the alarm and locking the front door, I drive home.

7 p.m. – Back at home, I lock my clients' house keys in the filing cabinet and complete the day's paperwork in about 20 minutes. Then, after pouring myself a glass of red wine, I settle down to watch *East Enders*, help or hinder my youngest son with his homework and cheer my husband on as he cooks supper.

10 p.m. – Bed. No trouble sleeping whatsoever!

Staying safe

One of the best things about petsitting, apart from working with animals, is the time spent away from the hustle and bustle that make up most people's working day. This is especially true of dog walking. But because of this environment and because we are often working alone, we have to be sensible and make sure that we are as safe as possible. So when you agree to meet the prospective client, get very clear instructions to their home and double-check times and make sure you've both logged your mobile numbers into your phones.

If you have any concerns about the area you might have to visit, then don't do it. Trust your instincts. If something feels wrong then it's better to pass up the opportunity.

If you are working alone – and most petsitters do – then write down in your large desk diary, all your movements for the day. For example:

☐ 10 a.m. Dog walking – Firs Common

☐ 11 a.m. Dog walking – Runnymede Park

☐ 12 a.m. Home

☐ 2 p.m. Dog walk – Byfleet Canal

☐ 3 p.m. Feeding Tigger – 11 Holly Tree Rd.

You won't have the time or inclination to write down full addresses and names every day but by putting the pet's name, your partner or friend can check through your diary to get an idea of where you might be at any given time.

When you are visiting a client for the first time, get a friend, partner, parent or even taxi driver (from a reputable firm of course) to take you to the prospective client's home and wait outside for you. Tell the new client that no, thanks, you won't have a coffee/tea as you have someone waiting for you. Keep your mobile phone charged and if you're on PAYG, make sure you have credit.

Some tips for staying safe.

☐ Lock your car every time you leave it. If you have the type of car alarm that can be accidentally activated by any pets left inside it, get it changed as a priority.

☐ Have your keys on you at all times. You can now get a personal alarm which attaches to your key ring. Don't be afraid to use it.

☐ If anything looks suspicious or if there are any signs of a disturbance – don't investigate, drive away and call the police.

☐ Your client should have written down the names and car registrations of anyone visiting their home in their absence. If someone claims to be a neighbour or friend 'just calling round', they probably are but don't tell them that the house is unoccupied.

☐ Carry a torch at all times.

☐ If you are unlucky enough to enter a house during a burglary, then remember that the last thing a burglar wants is confrontation. I always sing or call out to the pets as I'm unlocking the front door. This should alert an intruder and give them plenty of time to get out.

☐ If anything is missing or disturbed inside the house, get out and call the police. Do this even if something just looks 'wrong'. Trust your instincts and leave. Call the emergency contact and ask them to either check the house themselves or go in with you.

☐ Always call the police first and then the emergency contact.

☐ Familiarize yourself with all areas of the house which you have free access to. You should, on your initial visit, have asked to be shown another exit and been given keys to it. This is also vital in case of fire or if you lose or break another door key. See Chapter 8, 'Initial client consultation'.

◻ Consider having your partner, friend or family member put on your petsitting insurance. This is, with the pet owners' permission, so that they can accompany you if you ever feel anxious about a pet sit or visiting after dark. It also means that you can train them up to act as your emergency cover.

Deciding on petsitter attire and accessories

A waterproof tote bag is perfect for a busy petsitter. With this you can carry your pet visiting cards, clip board, sweater, and pet toys.

Some petsitters prefer a uniform and others wear casual clothes. I compromise by wearing combat trousers with a rugby shirt, fleece or polo top with our petsitting logo and web address embroidered on. I think a full-blown uniform advertises the fact that you might be visiting an empty house in the same way that having a permanent sign on your vehicle does.

You may want to wear old scruffy jeans because you think it's not worth wearing your best clothes for walking dogs or cleaning out rabbit hutches. It makes sense, though, to spend some money on clothes you'll wear daily.

Jeans aren't practical because they get very heavy when wet. They are not warm enough in the winter and are too hot in the summer. And they don't have enough pockets! Buy some trousers from a specialist company such as Regatta, www.regatta.co.uk. They dry in minutes and have loads of pockets – you can't have too many when you're a petsitter.

Layer your clothes because you can start off really cold but by the time you've walked for 40 minutes you will really heat up. I wear a tee shirt or a vest with a long-sleeved shirt over it and a lightweight jumper or fleece if it is really cold. You will quickly get overheated in a thick coat when dog walking, so a lightweight waterproof jacket is better.

Buy waterproof trousers to go over your normal trousers or shorts. Nothing is worse than walking with wet legs. These can be bought cheaply from school shops as there is no VAT on children's clothes.

In the summer, wear a baseball cap to keep your head cool, slap on loads of SPF 15 or higher to stop you burning.

In the winter, use a warm hat or cap to keep the heat in (70% of body heat is lost through the head) and if your ears get cold you are going to get painful earache. Loads of pockets on everything you wear are useful and a long-sleeved shirt is probably the most useful of all as it can double up as an emergency pet sling if your dog collapses after being bitten by an adder for example.

As I mentioned earlier, good boots are vital for the winter and spring. I get mine from an army surplus store. Rub some Vaseline into the back of the heels when you first get them to prevent blisters. In addition, keep polishing them regularly as this keeps them waterproof. As the weather gets warmer, you can change to trainers and possibly sandal-type trainers but be careful of getting scratched or, worse, bitten by an adder! A bum bag is something I'd be lost without. It should have lots of clips where you can attach leads, water bottles and integrated bowls. A good bum bag needs at least three zip-up pockets - one of them big enough to put a few vital first aid items in.

OTHER ACCESSORIES TO REMEMBER

Always, always take water, even in winter. If you ever get lost, you will be so glad of it.

Again, if you ever get lost and it starts getting dark, a small torch is vital. My torch is no bigger than a pen.

Either a rape alarm or a dog alarm will make enough noise to scare away an attacker or break up a dogfight.

Take a mobile phone with all those important numbers keyed in. These should include IDs for yourself and the dogs – woven collars, as I mentioned earlier, are definitely the best.

Spare dog leads – I tended to loop dog leads round my neck before I found some modern ones. An all-in-one lead is ideal as a spare as it's light and the more you dog walk, the more times you'll come across a stray dog. I've lost count of the number of dogs I've found over the years. More and more owners are microchipping so all but two were reunited with their owners after I took them to my vets or called the local dog warden.

I can fit a very light roll-up rain jacket in my bum bag which folds to no bigger than a purse.

It's useful to carry treats to entice stubborn dogs back or to buy you time when faced with an aggressive dog and no owner in sight.

After 3 pm in the winter wear anything reflective, and the same for your dogs. You can buy reflective coats and lights that fit on to collars.

You might like to carry a small bar of chocolate/and a banana. The chocolate will give you an instant sugar boost if you are feeling tired and weak and the banana, although, taking longer to work, will sustain you for a good while. If it's hot these will melt, so try glucose tablets as an alternative or if you're a chocoholic like me!

It could only happen to a petsitter...

For me, personally, I think one of the worst things that happened to me was having a large labrador chew through his dog/seat harness and jump all over me, causing me to crash my car and leaving me concussed. I left the car and started trying to walk home with Prince, the labrador, by my side. I managed to call an ambulance before passing out deep in the woods. Prince, meanwhile, ate my Ray-Bans which my brother had sent over from Seattle, and then 'guarded' me from the ambulance crew who had to bribe him with peanut butter sandwiches to get to me. They called the police, who put him in their car to take back to his owners but he vomited over one of the policemen's lap and then ate it all up again. Happy days!

10
CARING FOR HOME-ALONE PETS

In this chapter:

- ☐ Finding out about pets

- ☐ Meeting the clients

- ☐ Cats

- ☐ Dogs

- ☐ Puppies

- ☐ Fish

- ☐ Rabbits

- ☐ Small animals

- ☐ Birds.

Of course it's a good idea to study up on a great variety of pets before becoming a petsitter, but let's be realistic, most people take up petsitting intending just to walk dogs or look after cats. Sooner or later, however, you will be asked to care for animals that you know little or nothing about.

Unless you have worked as a veterinary nurse, a zookeeper or been allowed to keep a menagerie of pets as a child, you can't be expected to know everything about every type of pet. So when someone asks you to pet sit for their parrot, if you don't know anything about parrots say so, but say that you are willing to learn or to help find a petsitter who does.

Finding out about pets

I've always found that owners are only too happy to teach you what you need to know about their pets, but also, get books about parrots from the library, ask your veterinary nurse for leaflets and information, check out parrot websites and get as clued up as you can. One of the most gratifying things about petsitting is that you will be forever enhancing your education and your ability to help more and more animals.

When caring for pets in their homes, tailor your visits to the nature of the pet you are visiting. From the completed pet information form and your initial assessment of the pet, work out the most suitable type of visit. Bear in mind, though, that a pet's behaviour can be very different to that displayed when with its owner so you may have to adjust your routine accordingly.

Some basic things to remember for all pet visits.

- ☐ Fresh water must always be available to pets.

- ☐ Throw away any uneaten food and wash pet dishes daily.

- ☐ All litter trays and cages should be cleaned daily.

- ☐ Provide all services mutually agreed (e.g. watering plants, etc).

- ☐ Always spend the contracted time at each assignment.

- ☐ Don't allow into the house anyone who isn't on your visitors' form.

- ☐ Provide and complete a pet log or diary.

- ☐ Ensure the security of the property and confidentiality of your clients at all times.

- ☐ Try to see and, if possible, handle each pet at every visit to check for signs of illness or injury.

- ☐ Consult a vet immediately if a pet seems unwell.

Meeting the clients

At my first meeting with owners I explain that, depending on the type of pet, I will stay for up to one hour a day and offer feeding, grooming, litter changing and cuddles. Plus, I'll water plants, bring in the post and papers, open and close curtains, and generally make the house look lived-in.

Sometimes when you tell customers that you will be cleaning out their pets every day, their response will be 'There's no need, we only do it every few days' and 'well, what about the cost of all that litter or straw?'

You must explain – and stick to your guns here – that in their absence you will be the one taking responsibility if their pets fall sick and the most effective way of preventing many ailments is to keep their living conditions to the highest possible standard. You might mention that it's also more pleasant for their pets.

If they tell you they know of petsitters who will do ten-minute visits for a lower rate, you could try my standard reply: 'Well, that's between them and their conscience.' It is simply not possible to feed, clean bowls, change litter and bedding, check each pet for signs of illness or injury and play with them, in ten minutes. People who say they can I would not call petsitters: 'pet feeders' maybe but certainly not pet carers in any way.

> Always take a photograph – use your mobile phone – of any pet who you think may be ill or injured – for instance, a dog with his head tilted may be an indication that he has suffered a stroke overnight. Don't, however, let this slow down your journey to a vet.

Cats

When you get a call from a cat owner, ask if it is an indoor cat that uses a litter tray. If it is, then you'll have a much safer cat sit. If not, then try your best to persuade the owners to confine the cat to the house while they're away. I know some people may feel that this would be no different to a cattery but the cat can still have the run of as many rooms as its owner wishes.

If you think that's a bit hard on the cats, remember this: according to a 2001 Mori poll, 100,000 cats and dogs are killed or badly injured on our roads every year and more cats are killed in accidents while in the care of neighbours, friends and petsitters than at any other time.

Even if they stay near to their home, they may not come in for their food at exactly the time you are visiting. You are only there for an hour at the most so you could visit for days without even seeing the cat. If you can't see him or her, how would you know whether they were ill or injured?

Cats are creatures of habit and if they are missing their owners and haven't had time to get used to you, they may run away or find themselves a new home. This is particularly a problem with nervous or shy cats and is one of the best reasons for microchipping. A nervous cat that is free to come and go as it likes is a recipe for disaster. It may come, see you and then go, perhaps forever! To get the cat acclimatized to having a loss of freedom, the owner should be advised to start locking the cat flap and keeping the cat inside for a couple of days at a time.

Explain to owners, 'It really is for your cat's welfare and for your peace of mind that she or he stays in the house.' I give them this form:

Keep me safe, happy and well while you're away

Please lock my cat flap. If I use it, I may:

- *Disappear because I can't see my family*
- *Find someone else to feed and cuddle me*
- *Get sick or injured and not be able to get home*
- *Not be able to have a daily check-over to see that I'm in good shape*
- *Not have a chance to bond with my petsitter and miss out on lots of TLC .*

If all of this fails to persuade them, at least you tried.

When feeding the cat always follow the instructions given by the owners and try to make certain that he or she has eaten before you leave. A cat that doesn't eat can get ill very quickly with fatty liver disease so it's important that you know if they've gone off their food for any reason. Arriving at or shortly after their normal feeding time is a good way to try to make sure you see them; animals' body clocks are much better than ours, and there is a good chance they will be waiting by their feeding dishes. This might not always work, as some cats like to graze, especially when fed dried food.

It's a good idea when you first arrive, unless there are two doors between you and the cats, to push your tote bag or a noisy carrier bag through the door first, as some cats will rush to the door to escape the first couple of times you visit. They usually stop doing this once they realize that you are their personal cook, groomer and playmate. Throwing treats or catnip ahead of you, to distract the cat on entering, also works.

If you can't see the cat when you first go in, check your notes to see where its favourite places are. If you still can't find it, look behind sofas and under beds – your small torch will come in handy here. You only want to locate the cat, so if it is under a bed, don't try and get it unless you think it's unwell. Leave a couple of treats so the cat associates you with nice things and go downstairs to see to the food and litter tray.

Most cats are intensely inquisitive, so take cat toys with you, especially those filled with catnip and pretend to play with them or throw them a good distance away from you. Ignore the cat as much as possible and slowly, slowly you should get him to accept you. Even a cat who doesn't like to be petted or played with usually appreciates human company. He or she may be quite aloof to begin with but if you sit down on a sofa or the carpet, they may well decide to sit next to you or even on your lap. If they just keep you company for five minutes and then wander off, that's fine. Stay and read a book or check your diary. Enjoy chilling out. A cat may never let you stroke it but that doesn't mean you can't form a relationship with it.

MORE THAN ONE CAT

Multi-cat households can be great fun. All those cats interacting and playing is petsitting at its best, but there can be drawbacks. When you go to clean out the litter tray – you may find that there are cat faeces outside the tray – this is referred to as 'middening' and it happens because cats don't like sharing their loo area. If the cat owner has more than three cats and hasn't provided enough litter trays, cats may just stop using them and go elsewhere – in the most unexpected places. This then becomes an assignment from hell as you walk into a house reeking of cat faeces and urine. You would have probably noticed this from your first interview, so ask if every cat can have their own tray, otherwise think hard before accepting the job however much you love cats.

KITTENS

Kittens are sweet and adorable, but if they are younger than three months old then they are too young to be left by their owners. Kittens younger than six months old should be confined to a hazard-free room and warrant at least two visits a day, with three being ideal. This is obviously going to be more expensive for a cat owner and although many petsitters offer cheaper rates for multiple visits in 24 hours, remember that it is still your time and petrol and that, ultimately, it is the owners' dilemma and not yours.

Older cats are more prone to health problems and to depression if left by their owners. Again I recommend two visits a day or one longer visit. Try to keep to a routine as close as possible to the cat's usual one.

Ask owners of shy or aggressive cats, to buy a Feliway plug-in diffuser (www.feliway.co.uk).

This is a product which reproduces certain pacifying properties of cat facial pheromones and really does work.

Don't panic! It's completely odourless to humans.

AGGRESSIVE CATS

Aggressive cats are usually at their worst when you first enter the home so you could try and protect yourself by making a lot of noise, throwing car keys on the floor and, in a worst-case scenario, holding a bag or rug up in front of your face.

One of my clients had an enormous shaggy black cat called Cuddles who seemed to have the most sadistic sense of humour. I would enter the house calling him but he wouldn't appear. I'd prepare his food, clean his tray and then look for him. Every day he'd find a new way to scare the life out of me – catching my hair with his claw through the banister railings as I went up stairs, leaping out and nipping my ankles when I opened the living room door, jumping on my head from a shelf. He was just like the Pink Panther.

His owners had warned me. 'Cuddles doesn't like people. We don't know why but we've never been able to stroke him.' I resisted the urge to ask, 'Why name him Cuddles?' I kept to a routine of sitting down and reading with a catnip toy beside me and gradually he'd come closer and closer until, a few days before the owners returned, he was sitting on my lap every day. Of course the owners were amazed and it was so rewarding for me…and lovely for Cuddles who could give up his violent lifestyle. Always remember that an aggressive cat is usually just a scared cat; but always ask owners to have a cat like this, checked over by their vet to rule out a medical problem.

A good habit to get into is, after each visit, to leave the house as if it were your last visit. When I first started I would leave out things I was using the next day – dustpan and brush, hoover, etc. and even dishes soaking in the sink. Nothing that you wouldn't do at home, but when some owners came back early, I was mortified. I'd intended for them to walk back into the immaculate kitchen they'd left.

TOP-TO-TAIL CHECK-UP FOR CATS

You should try to do a top-to-tail during your initial visit. This isn't always possible as cats are often very shy with strangers, so I tend to ask the owners to do this prior to my first interview with them. Elderly cats – those over ten years – and those on medications should also be checked over by a vet before you care for them.

☐ Head – look in the cat's fur for signs of fleas – they are difficult to spot but their faeces look like black sand. Ticks are easier to spot as they are larger and either brown or – when they have ingested blood from the cat – grey in colour.

☐ Eyes – anything that looks sore, red or inflamed is cause for concern, as is a thick or yellow discharge. Some breeds of cats, such as Persians, do have a tendency for their eyes to 'weep', which just means a gentle daily eye clean for the cat. If the third membrane of the cat's eye is visible, this could mean it has a foreign body in its eye.

☐ Ears – normal earwax is clear but dark brown or foul-smelling wax may mean an ear infection or the presence of ear mites. A cat that repeatedly shakes its head may have a grass seed stuck in its ear canal. Only a vet should remove it as the ear canal is easily damaged.

☐ Nose – sneezing or discharge could be a symptom of cat influenza.

☐ Mouth – if the cat lets you, open his mouth gently. You want to see nice pink gums and tongue with no bad breath. If there are ulcers on the tongue, they may indicate kidney problems.

☐ Tummy – stroke the cat's tummy – if they will let you. Lumps or swellings should be investigated immediately.

☐ Back – if the cat will let you, gently stroke it all over. If the owner has indicated on the pet information sheet that her cat dislikes having his back stroked, then you would leave the area alone. A cat flinching from being touched in an area where he usually doesn't mind, might mean he has an injury or even a bite. Again check for ticks and fleas.

☐ Paws – the nails shouldn't be overgrown. If they are ingrowing, the cat needs to have them treated by a vet. Check for any cuts or sore areas on the pads of the paw.

☐ Tail – gently lift the cat's tail for signs of worms around its bottom. A tapeworm egg looks like a grain of rice.

Try to make your regular top-to-tail, part of a daily grooming or petting session for the cat. This will help it bond to you and be another reason why it will look forward to your visits.

Dogs

Normal, healthy dogs shouldn't be left alone overnight for more than a couple of days. They are pack animals and really don't do well if left alone without their pack leaders – the owners.

For a very elderly or sick dog, staying in his own home, with at least three visits from a petsitter, is preferable to being left in boarding kennels or in a petsitter's home. During my career I have looked after a few elderly 'home-alone' dogs and all of them were more content and safer staying in their own environment. The last one was a 17-year-old collie, Sammy. As you can imagine, I was very reluctant to take the assignment in case he passed away but his owners were called away urgently and the only other options would be to have him kennelled or boarded with a petsitter.

We managed just fine. I visited him four times a day, twice for walks and twice for just sitting in the garden watching squirrels leap from trees and deciding that it was too hot to chase them, although Sammy said that he could if he really wanted to!

Puppies

Something that is changing for the better is that more and more owners are considering their options when thinking about getting a puppy. I often have people phoning me and saying, 'we're thinking of getting a puppy and we know we'll need a dog walker – would you be available and what does it involve?'

If the couple are both out at work all day, I ask them to reconsider. They would be far better off adopting an adult dog who is used to being left for up to four hours at a time, and even that is far from ideal. Any good rescue centre would be able to advise them about the right kind of dog for them and they would offer after-care.

I usually tell them that I'm not free to look after a puppy, as I would have to visit a minimum of three times a day. When I then tell them the cost of three visits a day there's usually a sharp intake of breath. But a puppy takes up a lot of time at each visit and I am trying to put them off from even considering getting one.

Turning away lucrative work is one of the times when you really can prove how much you love animals and how important their welfare is to you. However, always get people's contact details and send them your bumph because if they do end up taking your advice and get a nice old gentlemen beagle, then you will probably get the pleasure of his company, which would be a treat for both of you.

If you do decide to offer a puppy service, you will need a dedicated puppy form and a list of things the owners should leave out for you, such as:

☐ puppy pads

☐ pet-friendly disinfectant and cleaner

☐ puppy food

☐ toys

☐ instructions on how to dispose of used puppy pads or newspaper

☐ games puppy likes to play

☐ D.A.P plug-in diffuser – similar to Feliway, this simulates a substance produced by lactating female dogs which may have a calming effect on dogs and puppies. There is now also a D.A.P collar.

Please don't consider taking on a puppy care assignment where the owner insists on crating the puppy. Crates have their uses – they can be a warm doggy den and a sanctuary, but if the dog is closed in for more than 20 minutes at a time, they turn into a prison. Crates should only be used when the owner wants to keep the pet out of harm's way; for instance, if you were washing the floor and didn't want the puppy to slip and hurt itself.

The bad news is that sometimes people will completely ignore you, buy a puppy and find a dog walker who will pop in once or twice a day and be happy for that puppy to stay locked in a cage for most of that time. You have, however, done your best if you make them aware of your policy, and that of the law.

Gwen Bailey, one of the most highly respected pet behaviourists in the UK and author of many excellent books which are, in my view, essential reading, has given me permission to reproduce the following article in full. Please show it to anyone you know who uses crates indiscriminately or who has been advised to use them by an expert.

❝ *Indoor kennels (wire cages)*

Indoor kennels are so easily abused that I will not recommend them as a matter of course. They can be a useful tool if used compassionately by knowledgeable owners, but in the hands of the uncaring, uneducated or the absent-minded, they can become a frightening prison for a dog.

Dogs have been designed by nature and bred by man to enjoy being active. Confinement for long periods of time can lead to terrible frustration, especially in young dogs and those from working breeds, which are those most likely to be crated because of their high activity levels. Their behaviour when they finally get free can be so appalling as they try to use up their energy, that they are quickly returned to the crate in an effort to regain control. If you have to use an indoor kennel, the absolute maximum for an adult dog should be 2 hours and this should only happen after a gradual and careful introduction.

When raising a puppy, it is much better to use a puppy playpen which has enough space for a sleeping and a playing area. This gives more space for the puppy to move about, play and chew, and, in an emergency, he will be able to go to the toilet if you are not there for some reason and he really needs to. Housetraining is not difficult if you know how (see 'The Perfect Puppy' chapter 7). Patience and vigilance are the keys to success and you should be there when your puppy needs to go rather than forcing it to hang on for a long time until it is convenient for you to take it out.

Unfortunately, there will always be people who abuse crates. There have been too many instances of people taking dogs to rescue shelters because they are uncontrollable and boisterous. On further investigation, the real reason is found to be that the dog spends nearly 22 out of 24 hours every day locked in a cage. Others have come in with bandaged front paws where their frantic attempts to escape have led to paw and mouth injuries. In these cases, cages have often been recommended by 'experts' in an attempt to cure separation problems when the dog is left alone. I find it interesting that we have sanitised the terminology we use by calling them 'indoor kennels' rather than wire cages which seems to make it more acceptable for people to use, and abuse, them.

If your dog has behaviour problems, get expert advice to help you understand the world from your dog's point of view. Professional advice from a member of the Association of Pet Behaviour Counsellors (Tel. 01386 751151) can help you solve the problem in a kind, effective and humane way rather than trying to contain it by crating the dog. In the modern world where there are enough restrictions on dog's freedom as it is, close confinement of this kind just to make our lives easier is, in my opinion, neither kind nor justifiable.

(Reproduced by kind permission of Gwen Bailey)

PREPARING THE PUPPY'S ENVIRONMENT

Ideally, a puppy should be left in a safe kitchen with a dog or child gate preventing him from leaving the kitchen but letting him see out.

During the first consultation with the owners, suggest they 'baby proof' a room for the puppy – i.e. no electric flexes that could be chewed, baby locks on all lower cupboards and sharp objects or anything which the puppy could harm itself on, should be removed. The room should be comfortably warm with a radio left on a low setting. Classical music has been proven to calm animals as well as humans. A pheromone adaptor – available from a vet and which mimics the calming pheromones of a nursing dog – can be plugged into an out of reach socket.

The dog's bed should be high-sided to prevent draughts and with lots of safe bedding, the best being vet-bedding which is synthetic, washable sheepskin used by vets for post-operative animals to rest on.

VISITING THE PUPPY

When you visit the puppy, don't make too much fuss of him in case he is learning to 'hold on'. Otherwise he will urinate inside the room when he might have been able to wee outside. By keeping your voice calm and gentle, you will not be conveying the message that the puppy should be excited or worried by the fact that he is 'home alone' and accept this as normal.

After feeding the puppy, put him outside again to wee and, hopefully, poo, offering lots of praise and hugs if he gets it right. Do this every 15 minutes, incorporating it into playtime.

The last ten minutes of your visit should be winding-down time. Gradually withdraw your attention from the puppy whilst you wash any bowls, clear up and do a last check for hazards. Fill out your daily log and check that the room temperature is neither too cold nor too hot. If it is threatening to get hotter or if the sun is going to move round and shine down on the puppy's bed, pull the blinds closed.

This may seem like stating the obvious, but often when owners leave the house at 7 a.m. it is very cool and they may have no idea how hot their puppy's environment could get. By the same token, in winter they will be probably be leaving while the central heating is still on and they are wrapped up in coats and scarves, unaware of how quickly the house will become cold – especially for a young puppy.

During the summer don't be tempted to leave even a top window open unless this is in your pet information form. A better idea, I've found, is to ask the owners to buy a really good fan – or two if necessary, before late spring. A free-standing one should be placed so that the puppy can't knock it over. A smaller one should be placed at the back of a kitchen surface or table, also making certain that it can't be moved or won't vibrate so much that it topples over.

Fish

Fish might seem easier to look after in comparison to dog walking or cat visiting but they still need to be fed and their environment monitored.

A FEW THINGS YOU'LL NEED TO KNOW.

☐ What species of fish are in the tank or pond? Are they freshwater, salt water, cold water or tropical fish?

☐ What kind of care do these different species require?

☐ How many fish are there?

☐ What is the daily routine, including the exact amounts of food to be fed? A 'pinch of fish food' to you might mean more or less to the owner.

☐ What should the water temperature be?

☐ Where is all the equipment kept? For example, the fish net in case you have to remove a sick or dead fish or put back a fish that's jumped out.

☐ Where is the fuse box and where is the electricity supply plugged in? You don't want to unplug a kettle and discover you've also cut off the oxygen supply to the carp in the garden!

THINGS TO LOOK OUT FOR ON YOUR DAILY VISITS

☐ Are all the fish swimming round happily or are any behaving unusually?

☐ Do any of the fish have wounds or torn fins?

☐ Does the water look clear and smell fresh?

If you do have to remove a sick or injured fish, wash your hands in unperfumed soap and put the fish in a small isolation tank or bowl – something that will be easy for you to transport to the vets.

If the owners are on holiday or not contactable it's a good idea to have the telephone number of the local supplier of fish. You'll find them very knowledgeable and only too happy to help out with advice in an emergency.

The most important aspect of fish care is your instructions from the owner. Make sure they are very concise. Owners are usually the experts here, as you will discover when you meet your first fish fancier.

Rabbits

I am not covering every aspect of every pet in this book as there simply isn't space but I will elaborate about the care of rabbits as I feel that they are one of the most unintentionally neglected pets in the UK, with guinea pigs a close second.

Rabbit owners seem to be divided into two camps: owners who have the most up-to-date knowledge of rabbit welfare and those who don't. Often the former will keep their rabbits as 'house rabbits', allowing them almost the same freedom as indoor cats. If they do keep them outside, the rabbits enjoy accommodation, which is usually much larger than any pet-shop hutch.

The second group often don't even consider themselves rabbit owners. They tell you that the rabbits belong to their children. I dread hearing this and have to bite my tongue to stop myself saying, 'You're the adult here. You are responsible for this creature's life so whether you supervise your children's care of the rabbit or you do it yourself, the buck – excuse the pun – stops with you!'

Nine times out of ten, it is pure ignorance on behalf of the owners and not deliberate cruelty. They tend to treat their rabbits in the same way as, when they were young, their own rabbits or guinea pigs were treated – housed in a hutch with a either a run attached to the hutch or one on the grass with the rabbit being put in it for exercise now and then. In the worst cases, there would be no run at all and the rabbit would spend its entire life in a hutch.

A good rabbit owner will nearly always have booked their rabbits into a rabbit boarding facility although there will be times when such an owner asks you to look after their rabbit for a weekend or when their usual bunny hotel is overbooked.

The type of rabbit owner who usually contacts you will, often, be the type keeping a rabbit in standards that fall below the ones set out in the Animal Welfare Act. This can be tricky for you.

The upside of this is that you have a chance to change an owner's way of thinking about how they care for their rabbit. This might take all your diplomatic skills, but you can do it.

SOME RABBIT FACTS

□ Rabbits live in groups and need the company of other rabbits. Keeping one rabbit is unkind. It will live a lonely life. Keeping it with a guinea pig is cruel for the rabbit and the guinea pig, who will often get attacked and injured by the rabbit. Rabbits need to live with other rabbits.

□ According to the Animal Welfare Act, rabbits need room to display their natural behaviour. They need space to exercise, somewhere to dig, to explore, to use those powerful back legs to jump and run. Living in a hutch with little or no exercise can mean they develop painful skeletal problems.

□ Rabbits need stimulation. This means toys and interaction with other rabbits and people. They need to gnaw, which helps to keep their teeth from overgrowing. Apple wood is ideal.

□ Rabbits are prey animals. They need protection from urban foxes, cats and stray dogs. Their hutches should be secure. Their runs should be made of steel mesh, not chicken wire.

□ Rabbits need protection from flystrike (myiasis). Flystrike occurs when a rabbit's bottom, (although it can be anywhere) becomes contaminated with urine or faeces. This attracts flies that lay eggs in the rabbit's fur. Maggots hatch from the eggs and, if left, will burrow into the rabbit's flesh. They poison the rabbit, who can go into shock and will often die.

□ The ideal diet for rabbits. In addition to a complete rabbit food in the form of pellets, hay should be available 24 hours a day. Hay is essential to a rabbit's good health, providing roughage that reduces the danger of hairballs and other blockages. Apple tree twigs also provide good roughage. Fresh fruit and vegetables should be given in small amounts as treats.

☐ Rabbits need a consistent diet so even if you feel that the food the owner is feeding is not adequate in terms of amount or content, you should discuss this with the owner and any changes should be made gradually to prevent serious digestive problems.

☐ Rabbits need to re-digest some of their droppings. These droppings are called caecoptropes and provide more nutrients for the rabbit when eaten again.

☐ Rabbits need very careful handling. Unlike guinea pigs, most rabbits dislike being picked up.

RABBIT VISITS

When I get a call asking me to petsit rabbits, I first try to persuade the owner to either book their rabbits into a rabbit boarding establishment or to take the rabbit to stay with other rabbit owning friends.

Before a client consultation with a rabbit owner, wash your hands and change any clothing which might smell of other pets, especially dogs and cats, so the rabbit isn't worried by any scent you may be carrying. Ask the owner to hold the rabbit for you while you do a quick top-to-tail check.

☐ Coat – sleek coat.

☐ Eyes – bright with no discharge.

☐ Body – the rabbit's spine shouldn't be felt through its coat.

☐ Nose – check for any discharge from the rabbit's nose.

☐ Ears – should be free of canker or foul-smelling wax.

☐ Nails – check that they're not overgrown.

☐ Teeth – check that they're not overgrown.

☐ Tail – look around the tail for any evidence of recent diarrhoea.

Ask to see the hutch, which shouldn't be in a draughty place or in direct sunlight and should have a run attached. The run should be situated on grass, avoiding plants and flowers which may be toxic. (Crocus, lily of the valley, foxgloves, leopard lily, burning bush, false hellebore, golden rain and lantana are amongst these.)

Is there a good amount of hay and bedding material? If it's winter, will the rabbit be warm enough? If it's summer, how will you keep it from overheating?

Explain to the owners that you will be cleaning out the rabbit every day and will need a good supply of sawdust, straw, hay and rabbit food plus fresh fruit and vegetables for treats. If they look aghast and say that they find cleaning the rabbit out once a week to be fine – that's not a good sign. Tell them that you can't take any chances with the rabbit's health and welfare and that you must guard against flystrike.

Do they seem genuinely fond of the rabbit but are just lacking in knowledge of rabbit welfare? If so, you have a real chance here to make a difference to a rabbit's life by educating the owners. If however, they continue to protest, I would leave them your brochure and some Rabbit Welfare Association leaflets and suggest that after reading them, they can contact you again for a second visit, if they wish. Remember to charge for subsequent visits.

If you feel you can help them, go through the paperwork with them.

If you accept a rabbit care assignment, here are some daily pointers.

☐ Maintain hygiene by cleaning out the hutch daily and throw away all bedding and food. This will help deter flies.

☐ Check the rabbit's bottom at every visit. Any soiling should be gently cleansed with either cotton wool and warm water or a special cleanser for softening and removing faeces.

☐ Clean and refill water bottles, checking that nozzles aren't clogged up.

☐ Let the rabbit have exercise in its run, or walk it round the garden in its harness for a least an hour at every visit. This is the ideal time to grab a coffee from your flask or, if the owners have agreed, make yourself one in the kitchen. You can then either sit out with the rabbit or watch it from behind a window.

HOW TO PICK UP A RABBIT

A study has shown that 'scruffing' rabbits – holding by loose skin on the back of the neck to handle them – can be stressful.

Anne Mitchell of the Rabbit Welfare Assosciation (RWA) recommends this method:

> *Put one hand underneath the front legs against the rabbit's chest and at the same time stroke down the rabbits back to the tail. Lift the rabbit by supporting his bottom and lift him quickly and bring him close to you so that he feels safe and secure. Some rabbits prefer you to tuck their head under your arm so that they are not able to see.*

Rabbit emergencies

☐ Bleeding from a wound or orifice.

☐ Hunched up.

☐ Diarrhoea.

☐ Breathing difficulties.

☐ Nasal discharge.

☐ Difficulty urinating.

☐ Squealing or screaming. Rabbits only do this if in severe pain.

If you detect any of these – get to a vet.

All rabbits should be vaccinated against: myxomatosis and VHD (viral haemorrhagic disease).

SOME EXCELLENT BOOKS ON PET RABBITS

A Hundred Ways to a Happy Rabbit by Celia Haddon

The Rabbit Whisperer by Ingrid Tarrant

The House Rabbit Handbook by Marinell Harriman

USEFUL WEBSITES

The Rabbit Welfare Association, www.rabbitwelfare.co.uk.

This is a hugely respected association and registered charity, which does so much to educate people about the care and welfare of pet rabbits in the UK.

Small animals

Guinea pigs, hamsters, rats and mice are just a few of the small animals you may be asked to visit. Before agreeing to care for small animals, find out as much as you can about that species' needs.

On your initial client interview for small animals you will want to know that the owner has provided the following for their pet:

☐ A good-sized cage or hutch – for guinea pigs this should include a run.

☐ A 'bedroom' for them to hide and to sleep in.

☐ Sawdust or wood shavings – whatever is suitable for the species.

☐ Water bottle – make sure you examine this to see it is flowing freely.

☐ Bottle brush.

☐ Exercise wheel.

☐ Wooden toys to play with and to chew.

☐ An appropriate disinfectant and cleaner for the cage or hutch.

☐ Bedding material suitable for the species.

☐ Hay for eating – for guinea pigs and rabbits.

☐ Straw for bedding – for guinea pigs and rabbits only.

Here are some points you might find helpful when you are a pet guardian to small furries.

HAMSTERS

Hamsters usually fall into two categories: syrian hamsters and dwarf hamsters. syrian hamsters are larger than dwarf hamsters and are often golden in colour. Syrian hamsters must never live or be placed in a cage with another hamster apart from when they are being bred. They will fight their mate, their siblings and their children – often to the death.

Your role should be to make sure the hamster can sleep in peace all day as they are nocturnal, be kept warm but out of direct sunlight, have fresh and dried food daily, be cleaned out daily and have plenty to entertain him.

The hamster should have a spoke-free wheel to run in as many hamsters will run up to ten miles a night. Make sure the wheel is of a good size as sometimes owners don't realize that a hamster has out grown too big for his wheel and may be hurting his back when using it.

Some owners have a plastic exercise ball, which the hamster is placed into while it runs around, protected by the ball. Although this stops the hamster getting lost – and they are incredibly good at escaping – these balls can be misused. The hamster shouldn't spend more than 10 to 15 minutes at a time in one, or not at all if they appear stressed or frightened.

You might find it easier to pick a hamster up by placing a mug in its cage and allowing it to go in it while you gently lift it up. Hamsters can bite if disturbed or scared so put your hand into the cage slowly and, if you do pick the hamster up directly, cup it into your hands rather than making a grab for it.

RATS

Rats often love being handled and make great pets, as they are happy to be awake during the day or at night. Many rats love a large wheel to exercise in, too.

All rodents can suffer from mites and lice so check their fur daily. They can also suffer from diarrhoea, which is often referred to as 'wet tail'. If you notice symptoms of this, then get the animal to a vet, as it is life-threatening if not treated quickly.

Birds

INSIDE OR OUT?

Pet birds will either live inside in a cage or outside, usually in a group of similar birds, in an aviary.

If it's the latter, then proceed with extreme caution as avian flu is a real threat with birds living outside – ducks, swans, geese and possibly those caged in aviaries, being more at risk. Check with DEFRA (www.defra.gov.uk) for latest updates and if you have any doubts, decline the assignment.

Pet birds are prey animals – unless you are asked to care for a kestrel – so when you meet a bird for the fist time, don't make eye contact. To the bird, this can make you appear more predator-like. Always take your cap or hat off when you visit a bird for the first time, as again, you may frighten it.

Learn what is normal behaviour for the type of bird you are caring for and for this bird in particular and, along with your usual questions, ask the following:

☐ Does the bird like to be handled? This is one of the most important things you need to know because if the answer is no, then how will you be able to clean the cage and allow the bird some flying time?

☐ Does it have any toys?

☐ Does the bird moult and if so, what is the owner's procedure for 'blood feathers'? (Blood feathers are the new feathers which appear when the bird has moulted, usually twice a year. The blood feather is just under the bird's skin and as the bird preens it pierces the skin, so allowing the feather to unfurl and grow to the normal length.)

☐ Does the bird like to be 'misted' from a spray bottle with luke-warm water?

☐ Should the cage be covered at night?

☐ Where are the cleaning materials for cleaning the cage? Ask for them to be left out separately.

☐ Is the bird frightened of anything? Some birds don't like bright clothing – ask them to be as specific as possible.

☐ Is the bird allowed outside the cage and, if so, how easy is it to get it back inside again? If the owner doesn't allow the bird out of its cage and you have been asked to sit for more than a weekend, then you will have to diplomatically remind the owner that you have to work within the Animal Welfare Act. The pet must have room to display normal behaviour and for birds this means flying or at least time out of the cage.

☐ What temperature should the room be kept at?

☐ Does the bird know any words or cues?

☐ Has the bird ever bitten anyone? If so, will you be able to feed and care for the bird without being at risk?

☐ What are the bird's favourite treats? (Not fingers, you hope!)

☐ What are the normal colour and consistency of the bird's faeces? You need to see them as well, because a change in faecal appearance is always a cause for concern. Sometimes something simple like eating green vegetables can make the faeces watery but you would always want as much information as possible.

TIP Don't agree to petsit for birds that have only just been brought into the owner's home. Allow at least two weeks for any illness or infection to surface. You don't want a new bird becoming ill on your watch.

TOP-TO-TAIL BIRD CHECK-UP

☐ Head – alert and looking around. If the bird's head is tilted up with its beak open, it may have a respiratory infection. Check also for signs of swelling, white spots or crustiness round the bill and the cere – the area just above the beak. These could indicate scaly face – a mite infestation.

☐ Eyes – full and clear.

☐ Feathers – clean, sleek, flat against the bird's body. Feathers that are fluffed up might mean the bird is cold or ill.

☐ Nostrils – should be clear with no discharge. Breathing should be light and regular. Wheezing, deep or irregular breathing may mean the bird has a respiratory infection.

☐ Body – should be upright and the bird should be on a perch and not on the ground unless picking up food.

☐ Tail – sometimes a bird's tail 'bobs' if it is breathing heavily – possibly indicating respiratory problems.

☐ Claws – check that they aren't overgrown and ask owners to cut them back if they are.

☐ Beak – like claws, shouldn't be overgrown and should be free from swelling, white spots or crustiness.

☐ Behaviour – a bird that was previously friendly and is now aggressive or shy may be sick. Sick birds may seem depressed.

Whenever you petsit for birds, either have a temporary bird cage or make sure the owners have one, in case of illness when you may need to take the bird to the vet, separate two birds or need a 'hospital cage'.

Your first rule before going into the house of pet-owning clients is to remove your shoes and put some different ones on. This will dramatically cut any chance of bringing in wild-bird droppings – one of the ways that pet birds catch avian flu.

Always wash your hands before and after handling birds and wear disposable gloves when you clean out the bird's cage.

When you enter the client's home and throughout your visit, chat quietly to the bird. Most birds love company and do get bored, so listening to your voice is comforting.

CLEANING THE CAGE

If you are allowed – and you are happy about it – then let the bird out while you clean out the cage. Make sure all windows and exits are closed off first and that no other pets, however friendly the cat is, are in the room.

Clean the perches daily as well as the bird paper and brush round the cage – or hoover if it doesn't distress the bird.

Put a change of toys in the cage and inspect any damage on other toys or rope ladders, mirrors and perches. Always check that the toys left for the bird are suitable. A toy designed for a budgie might have smaller parts which could injure a larger bird .

Check the faeces. Are they less than yesterday or none at all? Faeces mean the bird is eating so a decrease is worrying and you should make a second visit later on in the day or first thing the next morning, to check on the bird's health. See 'Bird ailments' below.

SAFETY POINTS

If you are house sitting for a bird, then bear in mind the following points:

☐ Teflon or any non-stick coated pans are highly toxic to birds. The bird will die within minutes if fumes are released from these pans. Not only pans are non-stick, other utensils can be, such as bread-makers and self-cleaning ovens.

☐ Scented candles, scented carpet cleaners and pot pourri can be fatal to birds so for safety's sake, don't use any of these products: no cleaning sprays, furniture sprays, deodorants.

☐ Avocados are poisonous for parrots.

Once the visit is complete, fill in your pet log, check that the bird's cage is secure and that it out of direct sunlight or draught.

Wash hands and change back into your outdoor shoes. I know this may all seem obvious so please don't be offended but it's easy to forget when you are rushing from one house to the next.

Birds are creatures of habit and will appreciate your sticking to the same routine for them although that routine needn't be boring if you liven it up with plenty of quiet chit -chat, games and a variety of food – from your bird information form.

BIRD AILMENTS

You will often see at a glance if a bird is sick. They might be sitting hunched up on the cage floor with feathers fluffed up and half-closed eyes.Other symptoms might be:

☐ weight loss

☐ low faecal output

☐ lack of appetite

- ☐ diarrhoea

- ☐ bloated tummy

- ☐ breathing difficulties

- ☐ depression

- ☐ sitting on the cage floor

- ☐ fitting or twisting of limbs/back/neck.

If you suspect the bird is ill, ring the vet for an appointment that day and then with disposable gloves on, gently move the bird into a spare cage. Turn the room temperature up and cover most of the cage with a thick blanket. Sick birds lose body temperature quickly. If the bird hasn't eaten, you could try soaking some bird seed in warm water to soften it.

When you go to the vet, take some of the bird's droppings with you. If the bird has diarrhoea, it may mean a stomach infection which may respond to antibiotics.

Clamydia or psittacosis is a serious, highly contagious disease that can encompass some or all of the above symptoms, which is a good reason for treating any suspected illness as worrying and why seeking immediate veterinary advice is so important.

As birds will try and mask illness, you may not notice something is very wrong until it is too late, so always be vigilant and follow the terms of your contract through to the letter. By this I mean the clause every petsitters should have in their petsitting contract: 'We will take your pet to the veterinary surgery if we suspect any sickness or injury and bill you.' Of course you can word it more diplomatically but that's what you should mean.

INJURED BIRDS

If the bird you're caring for becomes frightened of something and flies into a pane of glass, gently put it in a warm, dark cage to recover from both the concussion and shock and call the vet. Sadly, shock may yet kill the bird but you will have followed the right course of action.

Overgrown claws can cause injures if the bird catches himself with them or injures another bird, so if they are overgrown, trim them yourself, if you can, or weigh up waiting for the owner to return or taking the bird to a vet – which might be stressful for both of you.

Sometimes an overgrown beak will stop a bird from eating – trimming a beak should only be done by a vet or a veterinary nurse.

PARASITES

Pet birds living indoors are far less likely to suffer from parasites than birds outside in an aviary but there are some parasitic illnesses which you should be able to recognize.

Scaly face. This starts off as white spots on the bird's bill and then spreads round the face, forming a hard white crust. This is usually treated by a topical cream which should be spread onto the infected area daily for as long as the vet recommends.

Trichomonas is a crop parasite – in the area at the base of the bird's neck. The crop fills with air, making eating difficult, and the bird will often will regurgitate its seed or leave half-eaten seed pods around so that you may think it's eaten when it hasn't. The bird will lose weight.

Roundworms are common parasites, especially for birds which pick their seeds up from the bottom of the cage or aviary floor. A vet will often treat the bird for this in the surgery rather than dispensing medication.

If you stick to the mantra that every pet should be visited at least every day and that they must always have their water changed, food refilled, bedding cleaned out, ideally daily, and their exercise needs met as required by the Animal Welfare Act (see Chapter 4), you will be more than half-way to fulfilling their basic needs. You will be doing a better job than many petsitters and, sadly, some owners too.

11
DOG WALKING

In this chapter:

- ☐ Why dogs – and their owners – love dog walkers

- ☐ Asking the right questions

- ☐ Spending the first days with a new dog

- ☐ The lost dog

- ☐ Avoiding the dangers of pack walking

- ☐ Dealing with aggressive dogs

- ☐ Pooh corner.

Why dogs – and their owners – love dog walkers

How many careers allow you to spend your day walking in the countryside or local parks? What could be better than getting fit as you bond with man's best friend? For me it's not just the dogs that make dog walking so enjoyable. It's also rewarding to help owners who might otherwise struggle to give their dog the vital exercise it needs. To see the happiness on an elderly person's face when you arrive at their door to take out their beloved dog, who they can no longer walk, is immensely satisfying.

While there's no doubt in my mind that dogs who are 'home alone' need dog walkers, I asked Kris Glover, BBC Radio Berkshire's pet behaviourist and owner of my local puppy school, for her views.

As a pet behaviour counsellor I see a high number of dogs that are exhibiting problem behaviours in response to an inappropriate routine or environment.

'A good dog is a tired dog', is a saying frequently applied in reference to canine behaviour and training. As true as this saying is its opposite, 'a problem dog is often an under-stimulated dog' and often lends itself to our dogs acquiring less than desirable behaviours such as excessive barking, chewing of furnishings and garden digging, and more serious behaviours such as aggression, inappropriate chase behaviours and stereotypical behaviours, to include self mutilation.

Dogs are social animals and therefore have a high requirement for contact with us as well as a need to get rid of mental and physical energies. Therefore not only is a social animal, i.e. a dog, likely to suffer if isolated from other social beings for a large portion of its day, but also a lack of opportunity for channelling its mental and physical energies are likely to create problems not only for the dog but also for its family too. **,**

When a dog owner contacts you about walking their dog, these are the first questions to ask:

☐ Do they live within your service area? There's no point going any further if they don't but try and refer them to another dog walker who you trust.

☐ Would this be weekly or occasional dog walking? You will want to know if you can fit their requirements into your routine.

Owners will also often say, 'We need you at 12.00 p.m. every day.' What they don't realize is that that's the time every dog owner wants you. Never commit to a certain time. You never know what can go wrong in your day to delay you and you don't want to be held to your contract where you've stated you'll walk Max at 12.15 precisely. Give yourself a window of, say, between 11 a.m. and 2 p.m. If they use a dog flap or they'd like two walks a day, then 10 a.m. is fine but it is too early for a dog whose owners don't come back until 6 p.m. or 7 p.m.

You can plan your walks so that one week Jessie the Jack Russell gets walked at 11 a.m. and the next week, you'll walk her last at 2 p.m. That way all the dogs get a chance of being out earlier in the day.

As a rough guide, I wouldn't want any dog left longer than four hours and it's always better for a dog if he has his walk earlier rather than later because he'll relax more and sleep after his outing. Think of your dog. After his early-morning walk or potter round the garden, he has his breakfast and then the next thing on his mind is his main walk of the day. Once he has done this, his task is complete – until you come back at the end of the day and then it all starts again.

Asking the right questions

You can then move on to more specific questions about the dog such as: breed of dog, gender, age, castrated or spayed, dog's personality.

☐ Has the dog ever bitten a human? There would have to be a very credible explanation for this, such as someone hitting the dog.

☐ Has the dog bitten another animal or been involved in a fight with another animal?

☐ If yes, then what caused it? You'll want to give the owner a chance to explain – perhaps the dog had to defend itself.

☐ Other biting episodes? More than once? I probably wouldn't risk taking the dog on unless I was convinced that it wasn't the dog's fault.

☐ Does the dog have any medical conditions?

At this point, you would arrange a meeting followed by a short walk with the dog and his owner. I know some petsitters don't walk with the owner but I think it's vital to see how the dog behaves when it's out. How does the owner control or call the dog back? This is essential to see first hand, before you agree to even a trial week with you.

Once you've put the appointment in your diary, send out the information pack right away. This gives the owner a chance to read through everything and possibly to decide if you are right for them.

When you ring the door bell on your first visit, the dog will probably greet you before the owner! Ignore the dog. You're a stranger in his home and he may be feeling nervous and therefore react accordingly. Avoid eye contact and explain to the owner that you are showing the dog that you are not a threat to him and that you will 'talk' to the dog later. The owner will probably tell you that Bubbles loves everyone, but better safe than sorry. The dog will relax faster if you ignore him to begin with.

If there are problems and you feel uneasy, then don't take the dog on. Suggest they try a behaviourist and to contact you again once the dog is more confident and controlled.

If you are told that the dog doesn't like other dogs, I would personally tell you to decline. You will be putting yourself, other people and their dogs – and your 'walked dog' – in danger. You may also invalidate your insurance if you knowingly take on a 'fear aggressive' dog.

Spending the first days with a new dog

Walking one dog at a time is certainly best for a few weeks and certainly, every dog should have their first few walks alone with you and on a lead. When it's time for them to be walked with other dogs, plan carefully. Never let dogs meet for the first time in a car. They feel restricted and can't 'introduce' themselves properly. Let them meet in the open but obviously well away from roads. If you start walking and calling them to come with you, they should, after initial bottom sniffing, ignore each other and come with you. If you have problems, don't force the issue and keep one on a lead. You will have to walk them with different dogs, on a one-to-one basis or not at all. The walks may be for the owner's convenience but they are also primarily for the dog's enjoyment and their happiness and safety is your main concern.

Note: Get written permission from the dog's owner if you want to let him walk off-lead.

SOCIALIZATION

Many dogs have not been socialized well. Ideally this should have been done in their formative weeks, between 5 and 14 weeks, but if they have come from a puppy farm or a breeder who treats them like cattle and doesn't allow the pups in the house, they may be very anxious and tend towards nervous aggression. This can manifest itself in constant barking or running away when meeting other dogs and ignoring another dog's 'Back off now!' signals. Rescue dogs can sometimes be badly socialized. None of these things are the owners' or the dog's fault and by pairing the dog with a 'pro' or 'stooge' dog you can often work wonders as the more socialized dog will teach the newcomer how to behave.

Dogs are much safer if they aren't let off the lead but for many dogs – and dog walkers – this takes some of the pleasure out of the walk.

If you are not a dog trainer then you shouldn't offer to train the dog for a fee – you will not be covered by your insurance as dog trainers have to take on special insurance. The same goes for offering behaviour training for a fee. To give advice and be paid for it you would need to have professional indemnity insurance. This covers behaviourists and trainers in the event that they may give advice, which, for whatever reason, causes the owners to try to sue them. Always refer clients to a behaviourist or suggest they ask their vet for a referral.

However, with the owner's permission, you may need to enforce the training the dog should have already had regarding recall as this may say his life. Also, dogs forget training – just like us.

I always tell the owner how I train my own dogs to recall and then if the owner starts to do this – or any positive method – then you can reinforce this training during the walk. Do not spend more than ten minutes doing this with the dog, though, or the dog/s walking with him will get bored.

HOW I TRAIN MY DOGS TO RECALL.

I make the dogs want to be near me or return to me by giving them treats. (Don't give treats to deep-chested dogs because of the risk of bloat, which can kill in minutes. Whatever the size or the shape of dog, ask the owner on your first meeting, if the dog is at risk from bloat. Dogs that certainly fall into this category are: wiemis, vizlas, setters, great Danes and hounds). Otherwise praise them every time they come back. Whatever their age, but especially if they are under a year old, I hide from them just for a few seconds so that they get into the habit of constantly checking that I am still with them and haven't got myself lost. I also call them back to me during the walk, give them a treat and let them go. Sometimes I will slip the lead on for a few seconds before giving them a treat. This stops them associating returning to me with the end of the walk or that being put on the lead signals the end of their freedom – either of which is not fun for the dog! I am teaching the dog that to come back to me when I give one short command – 'Come' or 'Here' means a reward.

Don't shout or get cross with the dog, no matter how long it takes him to come back. Would you go back if you thought you might be shouted at? Always reward – you don't have to use food every time. In fact, some dogs aren't interested or some are so interested that they may jump up every time they return, so vary it with praise or throwing a ball or other toy.

Take a Kong with you. There are Kongs on ropes including ones, which float or glow in the dark. Make sure that the Kong or solid rubber dog ball is larger than the dog's mouth. If it isn't the, dog can swallow the Kong or ball, which could stick in his throat, blocking off his breathing.

No matter how good the dog's recall is, always put them on a lead for the last ten minutes of the walk. Leaving it until you are in sight of the road could be a recipe for disaster. Imagine a cat, squirrel or another dog by the road or, worse, on the other side. Before you can say 'Stay', you may have lost the dog. Think of safety all the time.

The lost dog

This is every dog walker's nightmare but in the worst-case scenario it's essential to have a plan in place.

If you lose a dog, go back to the place it was last with you. Wait 20 minutes and then call the dog warden, the vet (often the first place people take a stray dog) and the dog's owner. Even if the owner is at work, you must keep them informed. They will want to leave work and wait at home in case the dog goes there. Your 'walked' dog should be carrying your mobile phone number as well as its owner's.

If there's no sign of the dog after 20 minutes put the other dogs into the car and take them home. You can't keep them out for hours whilst you search, as they may need a drink and rest. If you can cancel your other dogs because they have owners home with them, then do so. Otherwise, let the other clients' dogs out for a wee break and don't charge the owners for that day. Explain what happened. They will understand because if it were their dog, they would like to know you were doing everything possible to find it.

If the worst should happen and you don't find the dog, then contact www.lostdogs.co.uk. This is run by volunteers and has been successful at reuniting many dogs with their owners. In addition put up posters in all areas where people walk their dogs as well as post offices, newsagents, door-to-door drops, radio announcements – anything you and the owners can think of.

Avoiding the dangers of pack walking

When I lived in Spain, walking home along the busy roads from whatever nightclubs my friends and I had bestowed our dubious custom on, walking alone was not an option. We weren't frightened of the dark roads, ghosts or muggers but the dog packs. These dogs were often abandoned by their owners and, left to fend for themselves, they resorted to their genetic imprinting and formed packs.

The packs attracted those too old and weak to survive on their own. In a pack they could eat what the leaders left. The pack leaders fought to maintain hierarchy by fighting any of those who challenged them.

This is often the behaviour of dogs who are walked in a large group (more than four dogs). Individually, they may be tolerant, sociable dogs but running with the pack, they can start behaving in a threatening and intimidating fashion towards other dogs and their owners. Not only these, but smaller, fatter or weaker dogs may get pulled along or bullied by the stronger ones. I would hate to think of this happening to my dogs and I am sure most owners would find this unacceptable.

The more dogs a dog walker has, the less control she may have, especially if she is inexperienced. If you have tried walking more than two dogs on leads, then you know that whatever contraptions you use, you are still left with the problem of having only two arms. Dogs and leads get twisted round each other and before you know it, one of the dogs has broken free and is bounding towards a busy main road. I have seen ten dogs tethered to a lamp post while the dog walker goes up to a flat to collect yet another one. Sometimes the dogs are bundled into vans with loads of dogs they have never met before. Imagine their stress levels.

With pack walking, the humans are the winners and the dogs, most definitely, the losers. The temptation to walk more than four dogs at once obviously appeals to those who love money more than dogs. For many of these dogs, the one thing they used to love – being out for their daily walk – is turned into a nightmare of choking collars and intimidation from their pack mates.

Dealing with aggressive dogs

If you are happily walking along and you see in the distance a dog on its own making its way towards you, then simply turn sideways and walk with your dog close to you but not on a lead. The fact that your dog has turned away from a head-on confrontation sends a signal to the rogue dog that your dog isn't a threat. If the dog comes closer, possibly holding his tail high, which is a sign of dominance, get your dog to sit – still with his whole body turned away from the approaching dog. Don't try to make a grab for this dog's collar to look at his name tag. If he is lost then he is will be on edge and the potential for a fight is high. Instead try to walk back to your car and report the stray dog to the dog warden.

If you feel threatened by the dog, throw some treats behind you at regular intervals while you walk. This should buy you some time so you can reach your car safely.

Should you or a dog you're walking be attacked by another dog, either spray the attacker with your dog repellent spray if you have it in your bum bag or press your rape alarm close to the dog. Don't put your hand in to try and break up a fight as one or both of the dogs may bite you.

Pooh Corner

If you are a dog walker, you have to pick up dog pooh. There is no way round it. It's vital that you do it every single time as you can bet your bottom dollar that the one time you forget, will be the one time you get reported.

The dangers of pooh being left lying around have been well published but on top of these, it's just nasty to tread in or worse, fall in whilst playing football. And, if you ever think you might be being followed by an unpleasant stranger, you'll have something unpleasant to ward them off with!

Your safety is a serious subject, however, so look after yourself by being vigilant and sticking to footpaths and well-populated areas. Keep your rape alarm where you can easily reach it – fastened to your belt or bum bag. Wear light reflecting clothes and make sure your dogs wears high visibility collars or coats.

Little things can mean a lot. Make a note of your 'cared for' dogs' birthdays and give a small present of some home-made dog treats.

I would tell you not to get too attached to the dogs you walk but I'm afraid it's impossible. You know they're not yours but you love them just the same.

12
COMMON ANIMAL AILMENTS

In this chapter:

- ☐ Common cat ailments
- ☐ Common dog ailments
- ☐ Diabetes
- ☐ Urinary tract infections
- ☐ Parasites, ticks and worms
- ☐ Vaccinations.

As a petsitter, the bulk of your work will be in the care of cats and dogs. This chapter deals with some of their common ailments, parasites and vet-recommended vaccination programmes.

The ailments listed below are by no means a complete list but I hope they will help you make informed decisions, should any pets you care for be affected.

As a rough guide, any pet who displays the following symptoms when you do your client consultation or during the course of your petsitting assignment, should be cause for alarm.

- ☐ Excessive scratching, which could indicate fleas, ticks, mange, ear mites or an allergy.
- ☐ Dull eyes and coat, lethargy, weight loss.
- ☐ Constant licking of the anal region, which may mean the animal has worms or blocked anal glands.
- ☐ Constant licking of objects can sometimes indicate diabetes.
- ☐ Excessive thirst and urination can be a symptom of diabetes.
- ☐ Any diarrhoea or vomiting which lasts more than 24 hours or if there are signs of blood in the animal's faeces.
- ☐ Limping or signs of discomfort when walking or jumping.
- ☐ Difficulty eating, or eating only on one side of the mouth, which could mean dental problems.

☐ Coughing, sneezing or wheezing, which could indicate a viral infection.

☐ Straining but unable to urinate, which may indicate a urinary tract or kidney infection.

☐ A high temperature.

Common cat ailments

CONJUNCTIVITIS

An infection caused by the *Chlamydia* organism.

Symptoms: Sometimes referred to as gum eye, the cat's eyes will be so sticky that they may 'gum' together.

Treatment: Soak a cotton wool ball in tepid water and, very gently, wipe from the inner eye outwards. Use a different ball for each eye. If there is no improvement within forty eight hours, consult your vet.

CHEST AND RESPIRATORY TRACT INFECTION

Symptoms: Wheezing, panting, difficulty breathing with the cat showing signs of obvious distress. If accompanied by a discharge from the nose and eyes, this may indicate influenza – viral rhinitis.

Treatment: This is an emergency. Get veterinary help as soon as possible.

FELINE INFECTIOUS ENTERITIS

The cat equivalent of canine distemper.

Symptoms: Loss of appetite, desire to drink but unable to do so, high temperature - sometimes accompanied by diarrhoea.

Treatment: This is an emergency. Get veterinary help as soon as possible.

Common dog ailments

COUGHING

A cough can be a symptom of a mild throat irritation but if it goes for longer than a few days, the dog should be examined by a vet to rule out more serious causes such as kennel cough or heart or lung problems.

EAR PROBLEMS

Ear scratching and head shaking are often the first signs of pain or inflammation in the ear. Ear wax which smells or any kind of discharge needs medical treatment. Sometimes a grass seed may lodge in a dog's ear, causing him pain and irritation. These can be very difficult for even a vet to remove so I wouldn't advise you to try it.

EAR MITES

Smaller dogs or dogs with heavy folded ears seem more susceptible to ear mites, which should be treated by a vet. Over-the-counter treatments often contain alcohol, which is painful on sore ears, and they are rarely effective. See also under 'Parasites'.

DIARRHOEA

Dogs often become 'loose' and unless there is blood in the stools or other symptoms, most dogs get better within 24 hours. Treat by feeding very small amounts of boiled chicken and plain rice. Make sure the dog drinks frequently and seek veterinary attention if the dog's condition worsens.

GASTRIC TORSION – BLOAT

Deep-chested dogs are most likely to succumb to bloat if they are exercised just before eating a meal or soon afterwards.

Symptoms: The dog's stomach will be distended, with the dog looking very uncomfortable. This is an emergency so call a vet immediately. See Chapter 13, 'Pet first aid'.

CONJUNCTIVITIS

This is common in dogs. The eyes look sore and sticky. To give the dog some relief, soak a cotton wool ball in tepid water and gently stroke around the eye. Use a different solution and cotton wool ball for each eye to stop the infection spreading.

LAMENESS

A dog may show signs of lameness if it has a cut paw or a thorn in its pad. It could also mean that it has twisted its leg while running or be a symptom of rheumatism.

VOMITING

Dogs will vomit after eating grass and often, like us, if they have minor tummy upsets, but if they vomit a lot in a short space of time or if there is blood in the vomit or if other symptoms such as a high temperature are present, seek medical help.

Diabetes

Diabetes is a condition where the body can't regulate blood sugar levels. Blood sugar levels are controlled by insulin, which is produced by the pancreas. Insulin travels via the blood stream, throughout the body, regulating blood sugar. Without insulin, the body's ability to store and utilize glucose is severely impaired.

The condition is manageable with insulin injections and or diet. According to Intervet (www.intervet.co.uk), approximately 1 in 500 dogs, and the same figure in cats, are diabetic.

In cats, most commonly affected are older, castrated males; most cats being over six and dogs over seven years old.

SYMPTOMS OF DIABETES

Even if the pet you are caring for isn't known to be diabetic, diabetes can, initially, be overlooked so watch out for:

- ☐ increased thirst

- ☐ increased urination

- ☐ excessive or greatly increased appetite

- ☐ weight loss

- ☐ lethargy.

CARING FOR A DIABETIC PET

As a petsitter, sooner or later, you will be asked if you can care for a diabetic pet. This involves making sure that the pet eats at regular times and only the amount of food stated by the owner on their vet's instructions. You will usually need to be with the pet first thing in the morning and late evening to prepare its food and administer insulin.

If you arrive at 7 a.m. one morning and 10 a.m. the next, you are running into danger time – the pet could suffer from either low blood sugar caused by lack of food, or too much insulin or high blood sugar, which can make the pet very sick. Stick to no more than a two-hour window in your appointment times with diabetic pets.

Some animals with diabetes are given insulin in tablet form and some have insulin injections. If you have not administered insulin by injection, then make sure the owner explains fully and watches you inject the pet. You should always make sure that there is no trapped air in the solution you inject, as this can be fatal. Even if you can't see an air bubble, fill the syringe an extra unit fuller and then push the excess back into the bottle until you have the correct amount in the syringe with any air dispelled.

Cats with diabetes should always be confined to their home when you care for them so that there is no risk of them missing a meal or an insulin injection.

Looking after diabetic pet is particularly rewarding and I promise that most pets hardly notice when you inject them. They don't hate you – honestly!

Urinary tract infections

Both dogs and cats are prone to urinary tract infections. These are infections of the bladder, kidneys and urethra. You may notice the pet straining, unsuccessfully, to urinate. There may be blood in the urine or the pet keeps licking its bottom. In cats this type of infection or disorder is preferred to as feline lower urinary tract disease (FLUTD). It may be brought on by stress and other factors such as kidney or bladder stones.

Prompt veterinary treatment should be sought, with antibiotics being the usual course of treatment if there is an infection present.

Parasites, ticks and worms

PARASITES

These uninvited guests can make our pets' lives a misery if they go unchecked and sometimes they can even kill. Pets should be on a good flea, tick and worm-prevention programme such as Frontline or Stronghold. These are usually squeezed onto the back of the dog's neck every three months. Make sure your client keeps up to date with this.

Ticks, worms and fleas were once regarded as a nuisance rather than a threat to an animal's health but we now know that ticks, for example, can spread Lyme disease, which can cause hepatitis B in humans.

Thankfully most parasites can be prevented from using our pets as hosts by a combination of veterinary products and preventative treatments. Whenever you visit a new client, always ask to see their pets' vaccination certificates and evidence of their pet's parasite prevention programme.

FLEAS: CTENOCEPHALIDES FELIS

These are nasty little blood suckers that rampage through a cat's fur.

Symptoms: Excessive scratching. Some cats are allergic to flea bites so even one flea will cause them a lot of distress. Test for fleas by combing the cat's fur and then wiping the comb across some damp loo roll. The black grit-like substance is flea excrement. The fleas are usually too fast to be caught.

Treatment: Fleas and tapeworms go hand in hand. Severe infestation may cause anaemia. Inform the owner that the cat has fleas and then take the cat to the vet for treatment. If the owner is going to be coming home within a day or two and wants you to wait, I wouldn't – because you don't want to get bitten too!

Advantix and Frontline are both highly effective preventative treatments which your clients can ask their vet to prescribe.

TICKS

Ticks, like fleas, are blood suckers. They can carry Lyme disease so it's vital that any pets you care for are protected. I usually recommend Advantix, available from vets, which repels the tick before it can bite and lock on to the animal. If you do find a tick on a pet you are caring for, either make the owner aware or remove it yourself – with the owner's permission. See Chapter 13, 'Pet first aid', for how to do this.

WORMS

Roundworms live in the animal's gut and feed off the contents. If they are allowed to remain, the pet will become undernourished and lethargic. Roundworms can cause vomiting, diarrhoea and weight loss, and *Toxocara canis*, the most common dog roundworm, can infect humans too.

A dog with roundworms may pass what looks like pieces of spaghetti in its stools.

TAPEWORMS

Tapeworms not only use animals as hosts, they use fleas as the go-between. They pass on the infested flea to an animal via grooming. The dog or cat licks itself, swallows the flea and then the tapeworm larva, inside the flea, develops into a tapeworm. The tapeworm then lives inside the animal's stomach where it grows and lives off the contents of the stomach.

A dog with worms may drag its bottom along the ground because the egg-filled segments shed by the tapeworm cause irritation as they are expelled via the anus.

Preventing worms: I use Drontal (see www.stopwormsdead.co.uk) and have found it really effective. This can only be prescribed by vets.

 Whipworms and hookworms are also common in pets who haven't been wormed. Hook worm is prevalent in many of the UK's foxes and can spread worms if dogs come into contact with their droppings. Again, effective worming treatments are essential. Avoid over-the-counter preparations as they are usually not strong enough.

EAR MITES

Ear mites are sometimes referred to as ear canker. The inside of the animal's ear will be caked with a dark wax or crust. Don't attempt to remove any of it but instead, take the pet for veterinary treatment.

Vaccinations

Dogs should be inoculated against:

- ☐ canine parvovirus
- ☐ leptospirosis
- ☐ infectious hepatitis
- ☐ canine distemper (hard pad).

And, if you are going to be walking dogs from different households, they should all be vaccinated against kennel cough.

All cats you care for should be inoculated against:

- ☐ cat 'flu (feline upper respiratory tract disease)
- ☐ feline leukemia
- ☐ infectious enteritis (feline panleucopenia)
- ☐ Chlamydophila felis.

All rabbits you care for should be vaccinated against:

☐ myxomatosis

☐ VHD (viral haemorrhagic disease).

If you live outside the UK, ask your veterinary practice for their recommendations.

❛ *It could only happen to a petsitter...*

Eindy, a petsitter with even more years in the profession than me, told me this story.

When I was a new sitter, I had a client called Felony, a huge vicious-sounding black labrador and his three kitty brothers. We played and romped and then I went to feed the cats and clean their litter box, which was in the garage through a door off the house. While I was there I talked to Felony through the open door but he wagged his tail so hard it slammed the door shut, locking me in the garage. I had my cell phone on me but my paperwork with the address of the home I was shut in was in the client's kitchen. If I called my son or the police and gave them directions, I knew that there was no way Felony would let them in. It was Thanksgiving and rather chilly. I ran water in the washing machine to drink and planned to use the kitty litter box if I need to! Eventually the owners came back and they thought it hugely funny and teased me terribly. Until it happened to them — so Felony and I had the last laugh. ❜

13
PET FIRST AID

In this chapter:

☐ Preparing a first aid kit

☐ Minor pet first aid

☐ Heat stroke

☐ Road traffic accidents

☐ Shock

☐ Choking

☐ Objects in the eye

☐ Burns

☐ Poisoning

☐ Adder bites

☐ Bloat.

First aid is literally the first aid given to a human or pet until a fully qualified doctor or vet can take over. This immediate help can save a pet's life or reduce the risks of permanent disability. Your job, in applying pet first aid, is to try to keep the animal alive until professional help arrives.

If there is a pet first aid course being run near you, then I recommend you get a place as soon as possible. As with human first aid, there's little substitute for hands on training. CPR (cardio pulmonary resuscitation) and mouth to snout (in animals, you breath into their noses), should be demonstrated to you by trained pet first-aiders. There is a real risk that you could do more harm than good if you aren't experienced in this aspect of pet first aid.

Preparing a first aid kit

Even if you don't intend to look after pets in your own home, it's best to keep a good sized, well-equipped first aid kit in your office. It can serve humans and pets with just the addition of a few pet-related items such as a muzzle.

If you haven't bought a ready-made first aid kit for your dogs, then you can make one up and keep it in your bum bag with the bulkier stuff in your car. Your bum bag kit should include:

- ☐ length of soft rope to use as muzzle
- ☐ adhesive tape
- ☐ cotton wool
- ☐ adhesive and gauze bandages
- ☐ sterile wraps
- ☐ plastic syringe
- ☐ eye drops or saline solution
- ☐ powder to stop bleeding.
- ☐ tweezers – large
- ☐ antiseptic cream
- ☐ styptic pencil – to stem the bleeding from a torn nail, for example.
- ☐ disposable gloves
- ☐ foil emergency blanket.

Even a limited amount of basic pet first aid knowledge, can save a pet's life. For minor injuries and irritations, you can make a pet more comfortable, for example, removing a tick or treating a cut paw. You will also be able to make a more informed decision about seeking veterinary care.

Minor pet first aid

TICK REMOVAL

Carry a tick remover in your first aid pack. These are small plastic hooks with two different sized slots to remove unfed ticks and those that have fed off the pet and so grown in size. I use the Tick Twister (www.otom.com), which you can buy from your vet or pet shop.

It's important to remove the whole tick and not leave its head inside the animal's skin. If you haven't managed to get the tick out completely, the area may become infected, so take the animal to a vet for treatment.

MILD STOMACH UPSETS

If an animal has vomited or has loose stools but otherwise seems well, feed it small amounts of cooked chicken and rice for 24 hours. If there's no improvement or the animal's condition worsens, seek veterinary advice.

BLEEDING

Light bleeding and minor wounds should be cleaned and/or covered with a dressing. Heavy bleeding which is spurting out is arterial bleeding. Put direct pressure over the wound while you take the animal to a vet.

Any bleeding that is sustained and heavy should be treated as an emergency. A wound that is bleeding profusely usually means that it is deep and needs stitching.

Try to control the bleeding as much as possible before taking the animal to your vet. Do not try to make a tourniquet as this can cut off the circulation from a limb. If you do need to apply pressure, in the case of arterial haemorrhaging where the blood is literally spurting out rapidly, cover with a gauze pad or cloth and hold it firmly on the wound for at least five minutes before securing it, firmly, with a bandage. Get to the vet as soon as possible.

Remember that animals in pain may bite, so apply a muzzle – unless the animal is choking or vomiting.

Of course clean bandages and dressing are ideal but if you don't have them on you, improvise. If you are dealing with a badly cut pad, then use a sock, glove, a piece of rag or anything you can find and really press down on the wound and keep it there with a bit of cloth or just use your hand if you have someone else to drive to the vet. Loss of blood is far more serious than a potential infection from a dirty cloth. The vet will almost always give the animal an antibiotic injection as a matter of course.

Heat Stroke

This is very serious and can be fatal. People forget that they can wander around in a t-shirt and shorts but a cat or dog has the same fur coat all year round and of course the darker the coat, the more it will absorb the sun.

Heat stroke must be treated quickly. Cool the animal down with water from your bottle. Pour it over his head if you are dog walking, making sure it's not icy cold though, or this will constrict his blood vessels and prevent the cooling process.

Soak a towel in water from the car or take off your shirt and soak it in any water you can find. Get the dog to vets at once. He may need to be rehydrated on a drip.

Don't dog walk between 11 a.m. and 3 p.m. on hot days unless it is by the sea or in a dark wood and only then for a very short time. Explain to the owner that it is dangerous. You must still be paid, though – you have gone to their house, let the dog out and decided that it is dangerous to walk the dog. The owner should be very glad that they have hired someone who knows what they are doing.

Road traffic accidents

Traffic accidents, when they happen, are fast and frightening and it can be hard to think rationally. Try to remember the three A's:

- ☐ assess the situation

- ☐ alert the emergencies services/vet

- ☐ attend to the animal.

If the dog you are walking runs into the road and is hit by a car, remember that the first rule of first aid is always to make sure that you stay safe.

If there are two of you or there is a bystander, get them to direct traffic and to phone emergency services and a vet.

Assess if you can approach the dog safely. Don't try to run across a busy road. If it is safe, then start talking in a gentle but firm voice to the dog and walk slowly over to him. Approach him from the front, if possible, so he can see you.

Any animal suffering from pain or trauma may bite so be careful, you may need to muzzle the animal before you can start any treatment.

You can always find something to use as a muzzle – a belt, a long scarf or a roll of gauze from your first aid kit – even a dog lead will do.

Hold the scarf under the dog's head and then tie it across its muzzle so that you are locking the mouth shut.

- ☐ Don't muzzle any animal who is vomiting or choking.

- ☐ Don't let an injured animal eat or drink in case it needs an operation.

Don't squeeze too hard, just enough to ensure the animal can't open its mouth. Then tie again under the animal's mouth. Bring both lengths of the scarf to the back of the neck and tie securely.

In the case of a cat or other pet or one of the short-nose dog breeds, such as a pug or bulldog, you can use a towel, coat or anything that can cover and wrap the animal completely. Be careful to keep enough room for air to flow to and from the animal's mouth and nose.

Call and speak to a vet before you attempt to take the dog to the surgery. The vet might not want you, especially if your description of the dog's condition suggests spinal injuries. You might also be directed to an out-of-hours or emergency vet.

Even if the dog can walk, any animal that has been involved in a road traffic accident should be checked over by a vet to continue treatment for shock and to rule out internal injuries.

Try to secure a wounded animal in transit, if you are alone.

Shock

Shock is a medical term for the body's response to injury or trauma. Shock can kill if not treated and is very often present in an injured animal. Always treat for shock as a matter of course after a serious injury, burn or choking episode.

SYMPTOMS OF SHOCK

□ Shaking.

□ Loss of body heat – cover animal with foil blanket, towels – anything which will help provide warmth.

□ Gums look grey, white or blue when they should be pink.

□ The animal appears confused and unresponsive.

□ Panting or shallow breathing.

□ Animal collapses.

To treat shock while arranging for immediate transportation to a veterinary surgery, keep the animal's airways clear, control any bleeding, and keep the animal warm and as calm as possible.

Choking

Dogs who chase balls, or worse, pick up sticks and pebbles, run the risk of choking on these objects. Dog walkers should never throw sticks as these can cause serious injury to the dog's throat.

If an animal is choking or gasping for breath, gently open its mouth, look into the back of its throat, using your small torch if necessary, and if there is an object, try to remove it with your large tweezers. If it's too large, don't force it as you may push it further down the dog's throat. If you think the dog has actually swallowed something sharp or dangerous such as a piece of jagged wood, metal or an old battery, then you need to get him to the vet quickly.

If you can't remove the object, it's blocking the airways or you can't see what the animal's choking on, then you'll need to try other ways or removing it.

For a dog, hold its hind legs in the air with its head hanging down. If it's a small dog, pick him up and hold him by the hips with his head handing down. Using this technique will hopefully make the object drop out.

> Never let an animal play with a toy or ball which is the same size or smaller than the animal's mouth.

For a choking cat, wrap it up in a blanket or coat to stop it moving so that you can try to look in its mouth. If there are two of you, one should call the vet for assistance while the other tries to locate any lodged object. Use your small torch from your kit to get a clear view. Any string or wool hanging out of the cat's mouth shouldn't be pulled out. Take the cat to the vet for safe removal.

Breathing problems should always be considered an emergency requiring veterinary attention, even if you can't see anything obstructing the animal's throat.

Objects in the eye

If you suspect that the pet has just some grit or an eyelash in his eye, then try flushing it out by gently pouring the saline solution from your pet first aid kit into his eye. If this doesn't help, put some bandaging or socks over the pet's paws to stop him rubbing at his eye while you get veterinary help.

Burns

Act quickly with burns. Restrain the pet and cool the burnt area with water, ice packs and a wet towel. Treat chemical burns with soda or vinegar. Keep pets away from open fires, pans on the cooker and electric cables, especially puppies and rabbits, who often chew anything.

Don't touch a pet who has been electrocuted until the electricity has been turned off. Don't leave chemicals lying around. Oven cleaner, battery acid and caustic soda are just a few of the chemicals which can cause serious burns.

Always consult your vet if any pet in your care has suffered a burn. Animals instinctively hide their injuries so a burn may be more severe than it seems.

Poisoning

Ensure that along with the other emergency numbers logged into your mobile, you have a telephone number for the nearest poison control centre. You will need to call them as well as your vet if you are concerned that the dog may have eaten something poisonous. Even if the dog appears fine, if you have seen him licking or swallowing water with another liquid in it or just a liquid on its own (yes, some dogs are that stupid) then still take him to a vet at once. Anti-freeze and rat poison (Warfarin) have no immediate symptoms but they can kill. If a dog takes a bite out of a dead rat, remember that the rat itself may have been poisoned and the dog will probably have ingested this too.

 Grapes, sultanas and chocolate are toxic to dogs. The higher the cocoa content, the more poisonous the chocolate becomes.

Adder bites

If you are dog walking on a warm day, you might be unlucky enough to encounter an adder. These snakes are often found trying to cool off by lying on footpaths and although you might not have seen a snake or realize that your dog has been hurt, if he begins to drool and tremble and his pupils dilate, then it may be that he has been bitten. Dogs are usually bitten on their faces but wherever the site of the bite is, severe swelling will quickly appear.

If your dog is bitten, don't make him walk. This will push the poison faster through his system. Try to carry him or if you are wearing a coat or shirt take it off and drag the dog along on it. If there are two of you, you could tie the arms of the shirts and make a stretcher. Don't leave the dog if you can't lift him, but ring for help.

Bloat

Gastric dilation, also known as bloat, is the name given for a stomach that has become very much larger than normal - filled with gas, food, liquid or all three. This usually leads to torsion, the twisting of the stomach, similar to colic in horses. Torsion can sometimes occur without bloat so the signs are even harder to spot. If left untreated, gastric necrosis and perforation occur. Death usually follows.

There are few things which can kill a healthy dog as fast as bloat. But you can take steps to try to prevent it happening to the dog you're caring for. To prevent bloat, don't feed the dog for one to two hours before or after a walk. Excessive drinking should also be discouraged. If the dog drinks copiously then this too needs investigation to rule out diabetes and other conditions.

Some breeds are more prone to bloat than others. These include:

- ☐ labradors
- ☐ setters
- ☐ pointers
- ☐ vizlas
- ☐ weimaraners.

Plus many others…you need to know your breed.

I would always suggest to an owner that a walk is scheduled well apart from feeding times.

14
RUNNING YOUR HOME OFFICE

In this chapter:

☐ Dealing with customer enquiries

☐ Steps 1–10 of a petsitting assignment

☐ Maintaining client files

☐ Respecting client confidentiality

☐ Keeping accounts

☐ Paying tax and national insurance.

In Chapter 5, I listed what I found to be the most useful office equipment and stationery. And now I'll go through the system I use for bookings and filing.

Dealing with customer enquiries

Following a phone call or email enquiry from a prospective client, note, in diary:

☐ Name and phone number.

☐ Location of caller…too far away? Give the caller at least one other good petsitter to call.

☐ Type of pet.

☐ Gender and age of pet.

☐ Is the pet neutered?

☐ Does the pet have any health issues?

☐ Is the pet on medication for any reason?

☐ Are there any concerns with aggression?

Having made a note of the above, you can now find out when the owners are looking for pet care. Again if you can't help them, recommend a fellow petsitter that you trust.

Having established that you are free on those dates, remember you still don't want to commit yourself to any visits before you have met the clients. See Chapter 8, 'Initial client consultation.'

Take down their full address and email address. Log it in your diary and say that you will send out one of your information packs. You can run through what is included in the pack but it can be a lot for someone to take in during one call. I usually say that I hope the pack answers all their questions but they can contact me at any time if they need more assistance.

Send out, by post or email, your information pack immediately. It's unprofessional to delay or worse – to forget.

As discussed in Chapter 8, my pack itself includes:

☐ A current price list.

☐ A pet information form, to be completed and returned either by post or as an email attachment.

☐ Terms and conditions. It's very important to ask that the owners read this thoroughly to make sure they understand them. On the day, you might want to reiterate the most pertinent ones.

☐ Petsitter checklist – a helpful list of things to have available for your use.

☐ 'How to leave happy pets' – A short guide to leaving your pets.

Note in your diary and on your PC when you sent out the pack.

When you receive the completed information form, either prior to your initial visit or during, put the forms in an A4 plastic envelope. Also put in the envelope any other information regarding these potential clients and then file it in your cabinet. When you do the initial visit, if they have returned the forms you simply pull out the file and take it, along with your diary.

If they haven't returned the forms, take new ones with you, in case they have lost theirs.

A couple of days before the visit call the pet owners to make sure they've remembered your appointment and, even if you are sure of the address, confirm the directions to their home.

Once you have a firm booking, fill out your client cards. Below are a couple of mine.

Front of card:

Mr & Mrs Turner
5, Heather Tree Rd
West Byfleet Surrey   KT29 FQE
Tel: 01932 67895   Mob. 077439780. Email. jturner@aol.com

Pets: Cats: Bramble Female 7yrs Bracken Female 14yr.
Visits requested: Twice daily between, 8-9a.m. and 8-9p.m.
Fees quoted: £10 morning visit, £15 for evening visit
Referred by: Jane Morgan
Pets' birthdays: Bramble. 12.01.02 – Bracken not known so send both cats cards in January.
Emergency contacts: Stella Green – Mum. Vet: Jan Patal.

Back:

Bramble & Bracken – Bracken: diabetic: 5.iu Insulin am and pm.

House alarmed.   Front door sticks – lift handle upwards.

Bracken may try to run out – use tote bag to block. No treats allowed.

Both cats friendly and like to play. Bramble likes a tummy rub.

All post goes behind toaster, out of sight.

Food: half can cat food – warm in microwave – am.
         Handful dried food – pm.

Owners request: bins out Thurs, 6 plants in kitchen water twice a week.

Make contact again with your new clients about a week before you are due to visit their pet, making sure nothing has changed that you need to know about: for example, the pets have had an illness, injury or trauma, the house alarm code has changed, visitors are expected that you weren't originally told about.

If any of your clients do acquire an extra pet, then you must always visit them and see the pet for yourself.

Steps 1–10 of a petsitting assignment

1. First call or email from client; decide from their responses to your questions if you are available and willing to care for their pets. Remember, this is not yet a confirmed booking.

2. Write all information down in your diary and fill out an index card with basic details.

3. Email or snail-mail an information pack.

4. Two to three days before your appointment, email or phone with a reminder and, if you have not yet received the completed information pack, gently remind them. If you phoned initially, send an email too.

5. The day of the consultation, make sure you have everything with you, including your portfolio and some petsitting contracts.

6. Returning from your visit, complete any paperwork, file in a new client folder and lock keys in a separate area.

7. A week to three days before the petsitting assignment, email or write to client saying you are looking forward to caring for their pets on such and such dates. If you have time, phone also.

8. Perform the assignment brilliantly, leaving a detailed log, feedback form, friendly note reminding the clients to text, phone or email you once they are home. Don't leave any keys in the home.

9. Secure house and take the keys home with you. If your clients are delayed, you might have to keep visiting!

10. Once home, file all paperwork and – if you haven't already been paid – send the clients an invoice.

If the client wishes their keys returned to them – remember to either charge for this or include it in your fees – request that they sign a form to say that they have received their keys back from you on such and such a date. I use a small invoice book for this and give them the top copy.

Do everything by email or letter even if you've spoken to the owners and confirmed the booking. You then have hard evidence if you turn up on a certain day and they say it should have been the day before.

Remember a fortnight's booking is not always 14 days. Add up each day and total it to make sure you are charging for the correct number of days.

Maintaining client files

In your client's folder, you can keep the following:

☐ Copies of invoices. If you use either an invoice book or pre-printed invoice pads with integrated carbon, then you can send or leave the top copy with the client, file your second copy in the client folder and keep the bottom copies in one place ready for your book-keeping days.

☐ The bottom copy of clients' pet logs.

☐ Printed emails and copies of letters, confirming dates and other correspondence between you and the client.

☐ Details of keys received and returned.

Get everything in writing.

The reason I suggest you email or write to clients as well as or instead of talking over the phone or in person, is that you then have a record – documented proof of dates, times, changes to routine – in fact everything concerning their pets and homes. It is too easy to answer the phone when you're half asleep or distracted by your own pets or children, and then either forget what's been said or misunderstand it. By the same token, you could ring a client to tell them that, say, you have a doctor's appointment the following week and that you can only walk their dog in the morning rather than the usual late afternoon walk.

They might completely forget and then blame you for their dog urinating on their new carpet because they didn't make alternative arrangements. In real life, you would have done your best to arrange back-up cover, of course, but having a copy of a sent email, you have proof that you let them know of your appointment.

Respecting client confidentiality

You absolutely must make it a rule to treat anything the client tells you as confidential, no matter how unimportant it appears to you. Clients and their pets do all kinds of fascinating things, some funny, some sad and some just downright unbelievable. If clients can identify themselves or their pet from something you've said which has got back to them – and they're offended or upset by it, they can cause a lot of problems for you. At the very least you will have ruined your relationship with them and lost their custom and, at worst, they could sue you.

All client records should be kept under lock and key and, if kept on your PC, password-protected. When ever a client leaves you, shred all hard copy and delete all their information from your PC.

Cover yourself completely by making sure that should you want to sell or throw away your PC, remove the hard drive first and take it to your local council who have systems in place to securely destroy all data on it. If you sell on your PC, you must clear the hard drive of any data which could identify your clients, past and present.

Keep all your clients' keys in a separate drawer to their records and label them by colour or another system. Don't put the pet's name on the key as all someone has to do is match the pet to its record.

Check with clients if they are happy for you to have duplicate keys. This means being even more security conscious but it does save a lot of anxiety and hassle should you get locked out. Remember, keys can bend and wear out. Plus, if your client loses a key or locks himself out – he can come to you. Not so great at 2 a.m. but a good selling point none the less.

Keeping accounts

Book-keeping is not difficult but it can be a bit of a learning curve to start with. An accountant will often give you a free half hour of advice so ring around and you'll find that they can offer a lot of help and will often save you money.

There is some excellent accounting software around which, backed up with a good ledger, such as *The Best Small Business Accounts Book*, designed and written by Peter Kingston with assistance from Stuart Ramsden (www.hingston-publishing.co.uk). I've always bought mine from WH Smith. There are two styles – one is the *Blue Book* and the other is the *Yellow Book*. The *Yellow Book* is best as it has a weekly layout with one page for each week of trading.

For accounting software, I use QuickBooks (www.quickbooks.com) and the starter editions of Sage are hard to beat. Within the QuickBooks software there are templates for invoices, which means you can not only send out professional-looking invoices, but QuickBooks will keep track of them too. If you have set up a business account with your bank, hopefully they will have given you three years' free banking. You might be given a year's free subscription to accounting software too. However, every bank is different and the market changes, so take some time to search for a good deal.

Remember, you are required, by law, to keep proper records for tax and National Insurance contributions.

Paying tax and National Insurance

If you are running your business as a sole trader you will pay tax on any profit that you make over the tax threshold. For example, in 2008, you may earn £4,635 a year before you must pay National Insurance contributions, and £5,225 before you have to pay tax.

HM Revenue and Customs have a helpline for the new self-employed: 0845 9154 515. Website: www.hmrc.gov.uk. You must inform them within three months of starting up as a sole trader, or face fines of £100 or more. It's very easy to forget about this, so write a reminder in big letters in your diary and calendar.

Have your National Insurance number to hand when you call them and the date you started business.

If you don't intend to work more than a few hours a week, then I strongly recommend you pay Class 3 National Insurance contributions. These are voluntary contributions of £7.25 per week and paying these means you shouldn't lose your right to contributory benefits such as an old age pension.

There are lots of websites which offer tips and ideas for small business start-ups such as www.enterprisequest.com and www.businesslink.com . You will find a more comprehensive list of all websites, organizations and reference books I've mentioned, in the back of this book.

If your business is successful – and I'm sure it will be – it won't take long for your annual turnover to grow to more than £60,000. You will then also be liable for VAT.

❝ It could only happen to a petsitter ...

Cathy Hamm was petsitting for a cocker spaniel who managed to get his rather chubby body stuck in the cat flap. Despite trying everything she could to extract him, he managed to pull the whole frame of the flap out of the door – dancing around the room with it stuck round his tummy. After 20 more minutes of gentle tugging, the little dog managed to get free – totally unscathed. ❞

15
TROUBLESHOOTING

In this chapter:

- ☐ Handling complaints

- ☐ Dealing with challenges with customers

- ☐ Making contingency plans

- ☐ Key issues

- ☐ FAQs

- ☐ When a pet dies.

Handling complaints

I hope that once you've read this book, your complaints will be few and far between. Let's face it though, in any business you are going to get the odd complaint or two. Just when you think you've covered all the bases, a client will bring up something which you hadn't even considered.

My first complaint came from a woman who, quite seriously, felt jealous and left out when her dog sulked on the days that I wasn't booked to walk him. The problem was that I have always tried to vary my dog walks to make it more interesting for the dogs – and me. This dog's owner walked the same walk every time so once we had established that this might be the problem, she too varied his walks and the problem was solved.

I had one complaint that I hadn't cleaned the kitchen properly after a pop-in visit to feed and play with some cats. I had, in fact, left the kitchen spotless but petsitters are not cleaners. We should, of course, always leave a house as we find it but our motto should be, 'Pets come first.' This particular woman was house-proud to such an extent that it became a Herculean task to care for her pets and I was spending more time scrubbing away imaginary paw prints than I was playing with the cats. This wasn't what I signed up for so I decided to be booked up when she called again.

I used to do an occasional dog walk for two very shaggy dogs. After returning them to their home one day, after a muddy March walk, I thought I had sponged off and removed all traces of earth from their hair. Unfortunately, I must have missed some which dried and then dropped off in lumps onto the owner's carpet. Later that day, I had an irate call from the owner complaining about this and asking me never to walk the dogs in the mud. I wanted to say, 'We live in Britain. That's asking the impossible.' But I bit my lip and agreed. However, I soon found that I was 'too busy' to help them again.

By leaving a feedback form, as discussed in Chapter 7, 'Petsitting business forms', you are giving clients a chance to mention a problem which they might otherwise not do. This seems like making trouble for yourself but a small problem can quickly grow and sully the image of you as a good petsitter in the clients' mind. You may think it doesn't matter which cuddly toys the cat has in her bed, but it might to a client – and the cat!

Dealing with challenges with customers

Make sure you know exactly what is expected of you by the client and vice versa. If, for example, you see a dog crate in the owner's kitchen, draw attention to your terms and conditions where you state that you won't care for crated pets. Nine times out of ten, the owner will explain that the dog sleeps there at night and is never locked inside it. If you're told that he wants you to shut the dog in the crate after your walk – refuse now. If you don't realize that this is expected of you until after you start walking the dog, then it's much harder to deal with.

Whenever it comes to the pet's welfare, be firm. If you have it in your terms and conditions that you won't walk dogs within two hours of the dog eating and the owner asks you to feed the dog after the walk, then refuse. It may be hard to do but it's much harder to cope with a dog who does get bloat after you've left him happily eating his huge bowl of kibble following a mad hour racing all over the park.

Getting paid on time is one of the commonest problems for petsitters. Your payment policy needs to be one you feel comfortable with and which works. You may have 15 clients and 14 of them pay you on time. One of them, however, is always a late payer who needs constant reminders. For you, this payment is very necessary to the running of your business. You rely on your income to pay for your petrol as well as your time, so any delay is bad news. For your client, paying you may come low down on their list of priorities. You have to change this perception. I am afraid that with some people, you will just have to withdraw your services. In your terms and conditions, you must state that not only non-payment but also late payment of your fees means a curtailment of your contract. In other words, you sack your client!

Making contingency plans

If you're a sole trader working alone, you definitely need a contingency plan – back-up. You will have times when you might be ill or want a couple of days off at short notice. You'll also need regular holidays or you'll suffer from petsitter burn-out. This happens when you work too many hours and have too few breaks. You're the boss, remember, so be generous with yourself and put a line through six weeks, at least, on your calendar. Don't take any bookings for those weeks.

If you have a partner who you can train as your occasional assistant, that's great. Just make sure you get them insured too, which should be around £30 – £40 per annum as a helper.

Try to network with other petsitters in your area and offer dates when you might be able to cover their workload and vice versa. Choose only petsitters who you would use yourself. Make sure they have valid insurance cover and are as knowledgeable as you. Offer to show them your portfolio and ask that they do the same.

Key issues

For such little things, keys can be a real headache. The problem is not only are they small but the whole security of your client's house lies in them. Here are my tips for well-behaved keys.

☐ During a client consultation, check that you can work both front- and back-door keys.

☐ Request that the client gives you a set of both – ideally two sets. The advantage to the client is that should they ever lock themselves out, they can come to you for a spare key.

☐ Make sure the client signs that he has released keys to you and that you get him to sign that he has received them back again should you return them.

☐ Don't accept requests to leave keys inside the house at the end of an assignment. If the client is delayed, you won't be able to care for their pets.

☐ Always try newly cut keys out before the client hands over care to you. Sometimes new keys have 'spurs' which need filing off to make them work properly.

☐ Locks and keys can become old and worn. Try spraying them with WD40 or wiping with candle wax.

☐ Don't allow clients to leave keys outside (under a plant pot, for example).

☐ If anyone else holds a key to a client's house, you need to know their details.

☐ Buy different coloured key covers and, using indelible ink, write the name of the client's pet on each one.

☐ Keep (in-use) keys secured to your person with a retractable key holder. These are metal circular devices which allow you to clip one end to your belt or bum bag, and the other end to your key bunch via a touch-retractable cord. You pull out the cord, unlock a door, and retract the key – all without detaching the key from you.

☐ Ask your insurance provider to add 'key loss cover' to your policy. For around £20 a year, you're covered should you lose a key and have to call out a locksmith.

I've twice locked myself out of a client's house. The first time was when I was dog walking a beautiful Irish setter called Ben. I'd let myself in, put the key down on the window ledge, made a fuss of Ben, clipped his lead on and out we went. As I pulled the door shut, I felt sick as I realized what I'd done. It was a Yale lock on the door so we were well and truly locked out. To make matters worse, my car keys were attached to the key bunch so Ben and I walked the four long, rainy miles back to my house to ring his owner. Ben didn't mind. Instead of an hour's walk, he'd had two and a game of chase in the garden with my two dogs. Luckily the owner thought it was hilarious – she'd locked herself out countless times.

FAQs

When training petsitters and dog walkers, many of the same questions get asked, so here are a few of them and my replies.

Can I petsit part-time?

Of course. It's your business so you can choose your own hours. Many petsitters start off working part-time. And this is ideal if you are going to offer a pet pop-in service because most of your visits will be to cats, who are usually quite happy to be fed and cuddled at any time of the day. You will find it harder if you want to do dog walking unless you can do this in your lunch hour. There's very little call for evening and weekend dog walking.

Do I need to be a registered petsitter to get work?

You may need to be registered or licensed with the council but you don't have to be registered with a trade association or any other organization to work as a petsitter or dog walker. I think the confusion lies with petsitters (who may or may not be council licensed) describing themselves as registered, which makes them sound like 'registered' childminders who have to be registered, by law, with their local council.

Should I charge more for a client who only uses me occasionally and rings me the night before to see if I'm available?

Yes. Absolutely. But instead of making her feel that she is being charged more, try explaining to her that you have a standard, *ad hoc* rate of, say, £15.00 per dog for an hour's walk. For clients who book you regularly for their dog to be walked for an hour a day, five days a week, you offer a discounted rate of £50 per week.

I was booked for a month's housesitting but the clients came back half-way through and now want to pay me for only two weeks. What should I do?

If you have it in your terms and conditions that you require notice (usually a few weeks for a house-sit), then the client should pay for the full month.

I've been asked to tap the nose of a dog I walk if he starts growling at other dogs but I feel uncomfortable doing this.

Again, make a point of stating in your terms and conditions that you never use negative punishment on the pets you care for. Shouting, hitting or anything else designed to cause an animal pain or suffering, however slight, shouldn't be part of a petsitter's service. Suggest the owners consult a pet behaviourist who is a member of APBC, the Association of Pet Behaviour Counsellors, or of APDT, the Association of Pet Dog Trainers.

When a pet dies

The longer you work as a petsitter, the more chance there is of you having to say 'good-bye' to an old or sick pet. It really is the last act of kindness that a pet owner can do for their pet when the animal has made it clear that their time is up. As petsitters we can offer a shoulder to cry on to those owners because not only do we know what they are going through but to some extent, we are going through it with them.

Julia Love of Doggies 'n' Moggies, found that she wanted to show how much she cared but couldn't find any pet bereavement cards, so she started up Rainbow Bridge Pets, (www.rainbowbridgepets.co.uk). From her online shop, you can choose just the right card to send your sympathy. I like to enclose a packet of forget-me-not seeds in with a card, too.

APPENDIX

- □ Further reading
- □ Useful websites
- □ Courses for petsitters
- □ Postscript.

Further reading
BOOKS

This is by no means a complete list but just a few of the many excellent books which are well worth investing in:

The Perfect Puppy by Gwen Bailey

The Rescue Dog by Gwen Bailey

Dogs, A New Understanding of Canine Origin, Behaviour and Evolution by Raymond and Lorna Coppinger

One Hundred Ways to a Happy Cat by Celia Haddon

One Hundred Ways to a Happy Bunny by Celia Haddon

The Greatest Dog Tips in the World by Joe Inglis

The Greatest Cat Tips in the World by Joe Inglis

Dogwise: Natural Way to Train your Dog by John Fisher

The Cat Whisperer by Claire Bessant

Make it Your Business by Lucy Martin and Bella Mehta, How to Books.

MAGAZINES

- □ *Dogs Today*
- □ *Dogs Monthly*
- □ *K9 Magazine*
- □ *Your Dog*
- □ *Your Cat.*

Useful Websites

☐ www.petskitchen.co.uk

TV vet Joe Inglis's excellent website where, along with his fabulous pet food, he also answers many pet owners' questions concerning their pets health.

☐ www.rspca.org.uk

A highly informative site which has fact files on caring for domestic pets.

☐ www.pdsa.org.uk

Again, an excellent site to enhance your knowledge of your pet as well as ideas for fundraising.

☐ www.dogstrust.org.uk

The best place for prospective dog owners to find a new best friend.

☐ www.cats.org.uk

The website of the Cats Protection League. A wealth of cat care information.

☐ www.celiahaddon.co.uk

Celia was the pet agony aunt on for the *Telegraph* magazine for many years and her personal website is packed with kind and sensible advice for pet owners.

☐ www.petcare.org

The website of the Pet Care Trust.

☐ www.doglost.co.uk

Run by volunteers, this website has helped hundreds of owners become reunited with their dogs. It also highlights the huge problem of dog theft in the UK.

☐ www.puppyschool.co.uk

Gwen Bailey's puppy schools are the ideal place for your clients to take their puppies for socialization, fun and education from highly trained and caring instructors.

☐ www.thepetsitting-news.com

A free online newsletter for petsitters.

Courses for petsitters

If you are interested in taking a course in petsitting, both the Animal Care College, www.animalcarecollege.co.uk and COAPE (the Centre of Applied Pet Ethology), www.coape.co.uk offer distance learning courses.

Many petsitters are now taking such courses and so, together with other 'accredited pet-sitters', I have helped to set up an Association for Accredited Petsitters, www.accredited-petsitters.co.uk, so that we can share information, support each other and raise the profile of this great profession.

Postscript

For me, becoming a petsitter has been one of the best things that has happened to me. I've had the privilege of spending almost each and every day with some of the sweetest, funniest and downright lovable creatures in the world. I know that many people dream of leaving their nine-to-five jobs and working for themselves, doing something they love. This is what my good friend Julia Love says about her decision to start a petsitting business:

> *My biggest concern was leaving a well-paid, secure job to leap into the unknown. It was when I lost a close friend to cancer that I got the wake-up call I needed and I left my job to set up my petsitting business. I figured, life's too short and I should give it a go, otherwise I would always think 'what if'.*

If you do decide to become a petsitter or dog walker, I'd love to hear from you. You can contact me through the *Petsitting News* or the petsitters forum – a Yahoo group.

Happy Petsitting!

INDEX